Country Craft Tools

Country Craft Tools

Percy W. Blandford

Drawings and photographs by the author

58154

GALE RESEARCH COMPANY
BOOK TOWER
DETROIT, MICHIGAN
1974

First published in 1974 in the United States
by the Gale Research Company, Book Tower, Detroit, Michigan 48226

Library of Congress
Cataloging in Publication Data

Blandford, Percy W
 Country craft tools.

 Bibliography: p.
  1. Handicraft—Equipment and supplies. 2. Tools.
I. Title.
TT153.B6   745.5'028   73-22569
 ISBN 0-8103-2011-8

Contents

5

Contents

List of Illustrations

PLATES

List of Illustrations

'How can a man become wise who guides the plough, whose pride is in wielding his goad, who is absorbed in the task of driving oxen, and talks only about cattle?

He concentrates on ploughing his furrows, and works late to give the heifers their fodder.

So it is with every craftsman or designer who works by night as well as by day, such as those who make engravings on signets, and patiently vary the design; they concentrate on making an exact representation, and sit up late to finish their task.

So it is with the smith, sitting by his anvil, intent on his iron-work. The smoke of the fire shrivels his flesh, as he wrestles in the heat of the furnace.

The hammer rings again and again in his ears, and his eyes are on the pattern he is copying.

He concentrates on completing the task, and stays up late to give it a perfect finish.

So it is with the potter, sitting at his work, turning the wheel with his feet, always engrossed in the task of making up his tally; he moulds the clay with his arm, crouching forward to apply his strength.

He concentrates on finishing the glazing, and stays awake to clean out the furnace.

All these rely on their hands, and each is skilful at his own craft. Without them a city would have no inhabitants; no settlers or travellers would come to it.

Yet they are not in demand at public discussions or prominent in the assembly.

They do not sit on the judge's bench or understand the decisions of the courts.

They cannot expound moral or legal principles and are not ready with maxims.

But they maintain the fabric of this world, and their prayers are about their daily work.'

Ecclesiasticus 38 : 25–34
The New English Bible

Introduction

Man is supposed to differ from nearly all the other animals of this earth in his ability to use tools—and what an enormous number he has invented and developed! For most of their time on this planet the majority of men have been closely connected with the land, with a reliance on the products of the soil. A large number of craftsmen have owed their existence to the need for experts to make and repair the tools and equipment needed to obtain crops from the land. Others have taken the products of the land and made them into things of use to man. Most of these things have been utilitarian, although often with a beauty of their own, due to fitness for purpose, but a few artist-craftsmen have been able to progress to things of beauty without regard to utility.

Books have been written about the multitude of country crafts. Some writers have given space to brief descriptions of tools and their uses, while others have somehow managed to cover craftwork with hardly a mention of the tools involved. No-one has attempted to approach the subject of country craftwork from the angle of the tools needed, yet these are vital. A craftsman, whether master or employee, owned his tools. In many cases he made them. His livelihood depended on them. He was proud of them and maintained them in as near perfect condition as possible. He did not lend them. The tools of his trade were often evidence of his skill and qualifications when seeking a new place. The beautiful, the durable, the strong, the workmanlike, the aptly-designed and the acceptable products of craftsmanship only came about because of the tools involved and the skill of the craftsman in using them.

This book is about the craftsman's tools, divided according to their uses and not their crafts. In this way it is possible to compare a tool for a particular action or purpose with others of broadly similar aims, yet employed in a different trade, sometimes on a different material. This approach allows the reader to visualise how something was done and to appreciate why a tool had a peculiarity when used in one craft that was not needed when used in another. Of course, there are some differences that are regional, and it might be difficult to find any justification for local preferences, but they existed and still persist in some places, despite mass-production and better communications.

No book of this type can do its job without plenty of illustrations. It is hoped that the line drawings and photographs will help the reader to visualise the tools and recognise specimens when he sees them. In many cases it is interesting to compare modern tools, produced with the aid of precision machinery, with the individually made tools which were common up to not much more than a century ago.

In the days when people rarely strayed far from the place of their birth in the whole of their lives, trends in one place had little influence on those of another place. Knowledge of a new tool or technique was slow to spread. When a local community was self-supporting and inward-looking, techniques and equipment were handed down and the size of a tool or its name became accepted locally. This is found by anyone collecting information on tools. In this book sizes are given against some of the drawings. These are only approximate and are intended for comparison. Other tools of exactly similar purpose might be bigger or smaller. If a man made a tool, which did not have any controlling size, such as the need to pass through a particular opening, he often made it to employ a piece of wood or metal of a particular size he had by him, without cutting it—he did not have a speedy machine tool to cut it effortlessly to some other size.

Names were certainly local. Some, such as 'hammer' and 'saw', were fairly general, although adjectives qualifying these tended to vary. The lesser tools often had more local names, which might be entirely different from the name given to a similar tool elsewhere. It seems almost possible to invent any name and find it used for a tool somewhere. What makes identification difficult is the use of the same name for entirely different tools, which is found in a few instances. In this book, the names which seem most general have been used, with other commonly-used alternatives quoted as well, but it is likely that readers may yet find other names which someone will declare to be the only true name for the tool. They are probably right in their own locality.

This book is compiled largely as a result of the author's own lifelong interest in and experience of tools, as much as in the crafts they were used for. He served a woodworking apprenticeship, complete with indentures, and has had a broad experience of all the woodworking crafts, as well as spending some time teaching art, metalwork and wrought ironwork. In recent years he has given his attention more to boat design, building and rigging.

Many of the tools described and illustrated are owned by the author. With a history of a family of country craftsmen in various trades, many of the tools have been handed down from generation to generation. Other tools have been unearthed from lofts and stores of interested countryfolk. Fellow enthusiasts and amateur historians have been most helpful. Readers may find that many country people can produce old tools if asked, and in some cases will not know what they were used for.

Of course, the best places to see and identify tools are museums. Many museums have far more available things than they are able to exhibit at any time. This means that displays are altered at intervals and tools may have to take turns with other items. One large collection of tools, always with some on display and a large reserve available to anyone seriously interested is housed at the Museum of English Rural Life, part of the University of Reading, at Whiteknights, Reading RG6 2AG. St Albans City Museum also has a good display of tools of all trades. Oxford City and County Museum has a display of tools connected with local crafts at their branch at Woodstock and Cheltenham Museum has a similar display. High Wycombe Museum has tools for chairmaking on display and many more in reserve. Bristol City Museum uses Blaise Castle House to display items of rural interest, although tools are not always on display. The National Museum of Wales, Cardiff, has a Welsh Folk Museum, where the equipment of various crafts is displayed. Many houses open to the public have tools displayed. One such place is Mary Arden's House, the home of Shakespeare's mother, a few miles north of Stratford-upon-Avon. A little further north of Stratford, the Forestry Commission has an open-air museum of country crafts at the Mayswood Centre, Wooton Wawen, Warwickshire. There are many other places where country craft tools can be found, but the author visited the places mentioned while preparing this book and found them helpful.

An organisation that encourages rural craftsmen today, and which can provide a directory to their whereabouts, is the Council for Small Industries in Rural Areas, 35 Camp Road, Wimbledon Common, London SW19 4UP. There is a similar service from the Small Industries Council for Rural Areas of Scotland, 27 Walker Street, Edinburgh 3.

CHAPTER 1

Craftsmanship

What is a craftsman? The term embraces craft workers of both sexes. Broadly speaking, a craftsman makes things by hand and normally sees the job right through from raw material to finished product. There are exceptions, but an assembly-line worker cannot be described as a craftsman, neither can the man who operates an automatic machine churning out identical objects. Both may be exercising skill, but it is not the skill of a craftsman. In some crafts the worker uses machines in addition to hand tools, but these are under his control and he has to exercise his craft skill in controlling them. An example is the turner and his lathe. Even with a modern power-driven lathe, it is the skill of the turner which produces results. He is using the lathe as a mechanised tool. In some activities the craftsman produces parts, which someone else uses to make the final object, but the parts he makes call for craft skill and each is an individual product. For instance, one craftsman made wooden clog soles in the woodland where the wood was cut, and another craftsman made and fitted the leather uppers in a workshop. In the chairmaking industry, the final chair was the result of the efforts of several craftsmen skilled in making parts.

In many cases the craftsman was also the designer of his product. If he was working to a design by someone else, there

17

was close liaison between designer and craftsman. It would be very unlikely that a craftsman would work to a design by someone remote from him. They would need to be in close touch. Nearly always a craftsman made things one at a time. Each was almost unique in that it differed slightly from all other articles broadly similar which the worker produced. In this sense a craftsman was also an artist, even if he was only concerned with utilitarian products.

The oldest crafts must have originated when primitive man, roaming in woodlands, used stones in the form he found them for cutting and hitting, with branches and boughs as levers and mallets. The same implements were used as weapons for defence and killing animals. Then, as man moved on to being more static, with some tilling of the land and the erection of shelters, some were found to be more skilled at these jobs than others and the first craftsmen found a place in the community. They did jobs for others and received services or goods in exchange.

The system of barter, or the exchange of services and goods, continued until quite recently. There was surprisingly little money in a village while it was generally self-sufficient. The carpenter did a job for the miller in exchange for a bag of flour, which he might then exchange with the butcher for meat. The blacksmith made parts for a wheelwright, who let him have waste wood as fuel. Assessing exchange values and accounting for debts due when they accumulated over a series of jobs must have been a difficult job. Even the vicar was paid in kind and his tithe barn is still found in many villages. Itinerant workers and those who hawked goods from the towns would want payment, and workers visiting towns would need money, but the close community in which most country craftsmen worked got along on mutual trust and a sharing of produce.

The discovery of bronze, then iron and some of the precious metals, brought primitive man further up the scale as a craftsman. The working of metal necessitated skill greater than the ordinary man was likely to have as a mere sideline to his agricultural and domestic activities, so specialists were called for. Evidence of remains from many thousands of years ago shows that primitive man not only made serviceable things, but decorated them, showing considerable design and artistic ability. From those early metalworkers grew the smiths and jewellers.

As wood is not so durable and wooden remains have not survived as well as metal, we have less evidence of woodworking craftsmanship, but some tools have survived and woodworking craftsmen must have had the skill to use them to produce work of comparable quality to the metalworkers. Wood was one of the most useful materials for many branches of craftsmanship, and still is, despite the proliferation of so many plastics and other synthetic materials.

Country craftsmanship in Britain is not entirely a thing of the past, but most rural craftsmen who are still able to make a living have had to move with the times and adapt their work so as to cope with 'progress'. For thousands of years, craftsmen practised their art with little likelihood of something revolutionary taking away their job. From long before the birth of Christ, country carpenters, smiths, masons, weavers and other craftsmen continued with little change, knowing that their job was secure in their community. There was a need for them and they thought there always would be. Son followed father, being assured of a place and an opportunity to earn a living at his craft. The country craftsman up to the eighteenth century carried on a job and served a need which his counterpart of several centuries before would have recognised. Even his tools were very little different.

So long as man was a local animal this condition survived. A few adventurers travelled and brought back ideas, but they were the exception. The conditions of roads made travel difficult. A few miles to a market town in summer was quite an adventure. The same journey in the winter was usually impossible. Then transport improved. Roads were made better. At the end of the eighteenth, and beginning of the nineteenth century, there was a fever of canal building. These, linking navigable rivers, made the transport of heavy goods over longer distances possible. Coupled with this was the development of industry. Factories in the Midlands began making goods that had previously been the preserve of the country craftsman. They began producing tools which previously the smith had made.

The canals were closely followed by the railways—too closely for the success of the canals, many of which did not survive. The network of railways brought communication to a bigger area, with transport of people and goods comparatively easy, so that people moved out of their village, either on visits or to work in the industrial developments which were crying out for labour. Instead of the community being self-contained, products from one part of the country were exchanged for those from another part. One part of the country began to specialise in a particular product and trade this for the products of other parts.

Even in medieval days in Britain, there were certain things for which a village could not be self-sufficient. Not many smiths could get their iron locally. Some of it came from the Weald of Sussex. More came from the Forest of Dean. Some came from the Severn Valley. The bridge at Ironbridge, still there, was cast locally in 1777, and the town named after it. Cloth, other than the locally woven wool, might come in via pedlars from Lancashire or elsewhere—pottery from the Stoke-on-Trent area.

One interesting example of what must have been early quantity production was the supply of staddle stones—the mushroomlike stones used to support barns or ricks so that rats could not climb up. These could have been made locally, but they were made in large quantities in the eighteenth century or earlier at the quarries at Portland and Purbeck, then shipped around the coast to ports where they were bought and carried inland to sell to farmers.

Craftsmanship

Most craftsmen were occupied satisfying the needs of people in the locality, but in this way they were doing little more than supplying a utilitarian product, with little scope for artistry or the development of greater skills and higher degrees of craftsmanship. The customers could do no more than pay for the essentials. Fortunately, some craftsmen were able to obtain patronage, which ensured them an adequate return while they produced articles of better quality. For many centuries the church was the largest source of patronage for promising craftsmen, so some fine examples of early craftsmanship in wood, stone, iron and precious metals are in ecclesiastical buildings.

Royalty and nobility also provided patronage. As the wealth and power of the church waned, this coincided with the growth of a class of wealthy merchants and traders, many of whom spent some of their wealth on the acquisition of furniture, gates and other examples of good craftsmanship, so the better craftsmen were able to use their tools on worthwhile projects.

Progress moved at a snail's pace for centuries. The order of things was little changed over a thousand years, then in just over a century the way of life of most of the world had changed. Little wonder that the country craftsman almost disappeared. Fortunately, one reaction to mass production is a realisation of the quality and attraction of individually made articles, so those craftsmen able to satisfy this demand are able to keep their workshops going. The smith has little call for shoeing horses, but if he can make wrought iron gates as a quality product, there is a demand for them. Potters, in comparatively large numbers, are able to find customers. In other crafts, some of the small numbers who have not deserted their workshops for the probably better financial returns of a soul-destroying job in industry are finding satisfying work in filling a demand now that competition is reduced. Saddlers have plenty of work. Farmers find there is no satisfactory modern alternative to the hurdle, so hurdlemakers have work.

Broadly the country craftsmen could be divided into several groups, mainly according to where they did their work. Those who worked in the woodland converted wood as they cut and moved on when the local supply was exhausted. The chair bodger in the beech woods was one of these. Despite the need for a lathe, his entire tool kit, including the vital bits of the lathe which could not be improvised locally, was very small. Similarly, the clogger, hoopmaker and others who cut spars and poles had very few tools. Next was the group of craftsmen who took the cut coppice wood to a workshop or yard and processed it there. People like the broom squire, rakemaker and gate hurdle maker had some homemade appliances set up, but their tools were not much more numerous than those of the first group.

Those craftsmen did work which called for little precision. A variation of an inch or so did not matter. Those who had to work more accurately needed an indoor workshop, usually with one or more substantial benches, with reasonably true tops. They all needed fairly comprehensive tool kits. While the coppice worker or the one who took the wood to a yard might double at more than one trade according to needs, the craftsman who needed a workshop was more of a specialist and needed greater skills. It was these workshop trades for which apprenticeships were served and trade secrets were jealously guarded. The smith was one of these specialists, with a place for at least one in every village. The carpenter was another. Although a specialist in one sense, he was expected to tackle an infinite variety of jobs. The wheelwright was even more of a specialist. Both these wood-workers needed quite large tool kits, their value representing a fair amount of a man's entire property. The cooper was another specialist woodworker, with a rather different range of tools, who might serve several villages.

Those who worked in stone and clay might be comparatively low-grade craftsmen, doing walling and making bricks, and needing few tools. The mason capable of decorative work in stone was more likely to be based in a town or itinerant, moving to where his skill was required. His tools tended to be heavy, so he probably had a cart or pack horse.

The saddler was supposed to need more tools than any other country craftsman. There was certainly a need for him to deal with harness and saddlery in every village.

Most craftsmen had their workshop set up adjoining their home. No-one went very far to work. Some carried on their job in their home. Spinning was a usual activity for women and looms for weaving were also set up in the home. Most static craftsmen could be said to live on the job which often meant working long hours. There were fewer distractions to take a man away from his work, but as most workers were self-employed and liked to describe themselves as master men, and incomes from their craft depended on how much work they did, there was an obvious incentive to keep at it. Even then, the return from the work was not much, by present day standards, and the agricultural workers fared even worse.

It is interesting to see that the development of crafts followed very similar patterns in other parts of the world although at different paces. In America, of course, craftsmen emigrated from Europe and the need for specialists in the various trades was met in American pioneering days in the same way as in Britain. Improved transport and communications, with possibly a quicker industrialisation, killed country craftsmanship more definitely there than in Britain. The lack of individual craft skills is now seen in the demand for craft products in America from Britain and the rest of Europe.

European progress has been much the same as in Britain, although some countries have hung on to craft skills. For instance, wood carving is still a profitable cottage industry in parts of Switzerland, Austria and Germany. Much of the craft-work developments in Britain came with the Roman invasion. At that time, around the birth date of Christ, much of Europe was under Roman domination so crafts of similar types and techniques were started in those parts of Europe which formed the Roman Empire.

Elsewhere it is possible to see craftwork developments several centuries behind our own experience. In India excellent woodwork and metalwork is being done with most primitive tools and equipment. In many parts of Africa the natives are having to try to move from something like the Stone Age to the Atomic Age in one generation, so primitive tools are still found in use not far from the most modern machinery. In Japan the whole thing may be seen taken to what might be called its illogical conclusion, with all pretence of individual craftsmanship giving way to all-out industrialism.

CHAPTER 2

Axes

Primitive man probably picked up a stone with a sharp edge and used it both as a weapon and as a tool for skinning animals, splitting wood or digging soil. He would soon discover that some stones were more suitable and would keep sharp strong edges, while others were weak and would crumble. Flint proved to be his standby in North America, Wales and other places where he could find it. It may not have been long before he discovered that he could get more power into a blow by fixing the stone to a handle. The mechanics of it may have been beyond him, but having the heavy head further from the fulcrum of his wrist, elbow or shoulder, allowed the cutting edge to be brought down with more force. And so the axe was born.

Lashing the stone head to a wood shaft was obviously not very satisfactory, although that must have been the first method used. As skill developed, the shaft was put through a hole in the axe head. Making a hole seems to have been achieved quite early in tool history, possibly by slow work with another stone, as may be seen by examples discovered. One is the olerine dolerite axe head of the late Bronze Age, about 1000BC, in the museum at Wookey Hole. Although worn away by water, it was obviously quite a good shape (Fig 1A). This is still the most favoured method of attachment, although the risk of the parts

25

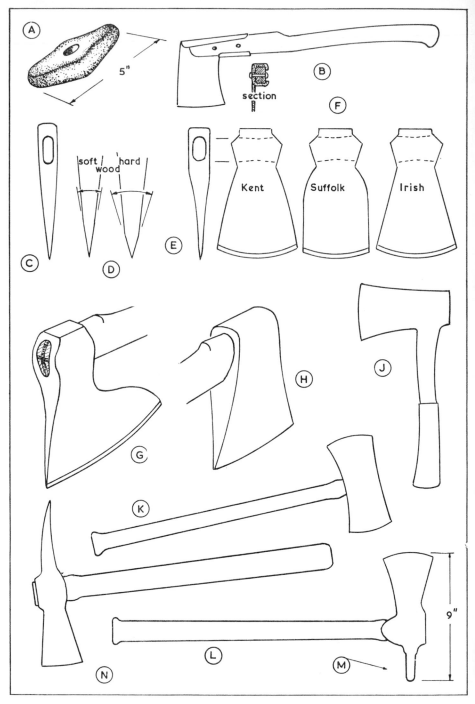

Fig 1 Axes: early and localised types

separating, with possible dire consequences, has not yet been completely eliminated.

In the Middle Ages some country craftsmen may not have had the skill to put a hole in a steel axe head. An alternative was to wrap the steel of the head around the shaft, making a folded socket, secured by rivets—not such a workmanlike method, but apparently satisfactory (Fig 1B).

To the uninitiated there would not seem to be many possible variations in axe design, but in fact there have been an enormous variety over the years and even in these days of mass production and apparent uniformity, there are still local preferences. Axe and hatchet heads differ between America and Europe. In Britain certain districts favour particular shapes. Even the method of hafting varies. For instance, a Warwickshire craftsman recently bought a felling axe with the generally-acceptable dog-leg haft, and replaced this with a straight haft made from one intended for a pick-axe.

In earlier days, much of the reason for variety in the design of axes, and other tools, was due to local manufacture in a small community isolated almost completely except for occasional travellers and rare visits to a market town. Like many other tools, an axe is a personal item and once a craftsman is used to one axe he may not want to use another, even of the same type, and certainly would not welcome one of an entirely different pattern.

An axe has two actions—it cuts and splits. The edge needs to be sharp so as to start a cut, but the wedge shape behind the cutting edge follows through and opens the cut (Fig 1C). How acutely the cutting edge is shaped depends to a certain extent on the wood to be cut. A fine (acute) edge might stand up to work on softwoods such as spruce and fir for some time, but would soon blunt on hardwoods, so for oak, elm and other hardwoods the edge would be given a more obtuse angle (Fig 1D).

For light work, such as trimming twigs and small branches

27

or chopping firewood, the thickening to give a splitting action may not be so necessary. Some axes were almost parallel in their thickness behind the edge, but an axe for tree felling or logging and similar heavier work depends as much on the wedge section as on the sharpness of the edge. In some places the words 'axe' and 'hatchet' seem to be interchangeable. In Britain a one-handed tool today tends to be called a 'hand axe', while the two-handed tool is a 'felling axe'. In the USA a one-handed tool is more commonly a 'hatchet' and the two-handed tool an 'axe'. The word 'hatchet' is used in Britain, but it is most often applied to an axe which has little taper behind the cutting edge (Fig 1E).

Most axes of British traditional form were made with a side view showing the blade curving in below the socket, then the cheeks each side of the socket broadened. Even this basic form had many local variations (Fig 1F) and these have not yet completely died out. For the lighter crafts, such as rake and besom broom making, the blade had a longer straight or curved cutting edge than for general forestry work. The coach builder also favoured an axe with a very long cutting edge, being shaped to extend towards the handle (Fig 1G). The now more popular 'hunter' type of axe head (Fig 1H) is more streamlined. This seems to have originated in America—it certainly achieved its early popularity there.

Except for primitive man's attempts at axe making with stone and bronze or other early metals, axe heads have always been made of steel. A snag with manufacture by a blacksmith or local small industry would have been the difficulty of hardening and tempering (see Appendix 1). To obtain the correct temper at the cutting edge by the methods available, would mean the rest of the head would be soft. Perhaps $\frac{1}{2}$in back from the cutting edge would be satisfactory, but once the edge had been worn and ground that far back, the steel would be too soft to retain a good edge and the head would have to be rehardened and tempered—a process complicated by the need to remove and replace the haft, so that it did not suffer from heat.

The 'haft' (shaft, handle) had to be strong enough to resist shock every time a blow was struck and springy enough to do this and cushion the shock on the user's arms. The British wood best able to do this has always been ash. Fortunately ash has been widely distributed and plentiful, as it has been in great demand for wheelwrights' work and many other things besides tool handles. The only other wood satisfactory for the purpose is hickory. This is more common in the USA, but not much of this is native to Britain, so hickory would not have become as common as it is today for axe handles until the coming of easier overseas trade and the import of timber in bulk. Hickory is closer-grained and generally of better appearance. but functionally there seems little to choose between the woods.

Wood as a natural product varies in its characteristics, so that strength and quality may vary between handles. Uniformity of quality of materials is an important consideration in quantity production. In an attempt to achieve this some modern hand axes have been made of steel with the handle and head all in one piece (Fig 1J). An attempt to cushion the shock on the hand is made by providing a rubber grip. This one-piece construction also removes the risk of a head flying off, but it is unlikely that any serious user of axes would accept this type.

The obvious basic shape of handle is straight. Many early axes would have had a crude piece of natural wood of no particular shape fitted to the head. In some places a straight handle is still favoured, but most craftsmen prefer some shaping in the handle. The handle has to be straight in those tools where both sides of the head are used. The double-bladed felling axe is an example (Fig 1K). This seemingly dangerous tool has never found much acceptance in Britain, but it is used for tree-felling and topping in America. The great advantage, of course, is in having two cutting edges available before sharpening is needed, so that a worker, possibly on piecework up high amongst branches, does not need to delay or stop for sharpening.

Another two-sided axe with a straight handle was the slaughterer's pole axe (Fig 1L). This had a normal axe blade on one side, but the deadly part was the pole extending from the other side which was used to stun by piercing the front of the skull of an animal (Fig 1M).

An ice axe also had a straight blade. The value of ice for preserving food was known from at least the early nineteenth century, when country estates had ice houses (favoured in America) or pits or caves (more usual in Britain). Winter ice from rivers and lakes was used for as long as it would last into the summer. The tool that was used to trim blocks of ice was two-handed, with a long thin blade and a pick at the other side (Fig 1N).

The shaping of axe handles would have been done with another axe and later with a draw knife. The modern 'dog-leg' shape must have evolved in many places out of touch with each other, yet similar results came as an application of fitness for purpose, as can be seen in many surviving specimens. Today, the dog-leg may have its double bend slight (Fig 2A) or pronounced (Fig 2B). Too much curvature might cut across lines of grain and be a source of weakness. The individual craftsman would have picked a piece of wood with enough twist in the grain to follow the shape of the handle—something not possible in quantity production.

Traditional axes mostly had the end of the handle parallel in width or even tapered, but from early days the value of an elliptical section was appreciated. The axe could then be held the right way by feel. Thickening the end of the handle to give a pronounced heel and toe is a safety precaution, as it prevents the axe pulling out of the hand by centrifugal force (Fig 2C). Modern axes nearly always have this, although some hatchets may not. It complicates production and involves starting with

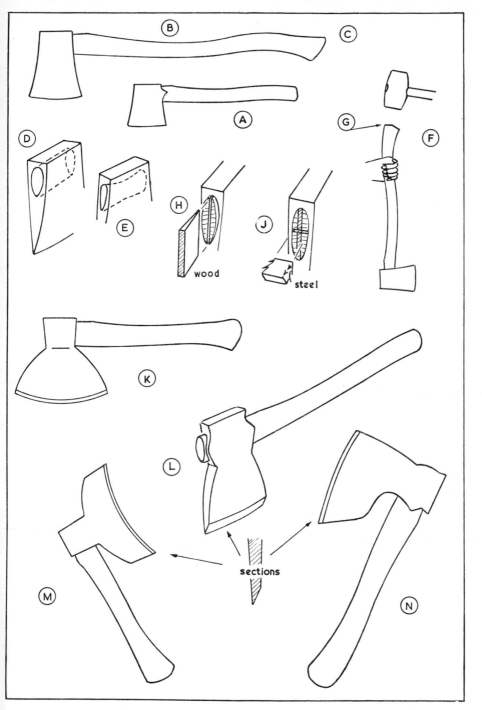

Fig 2 Axes: construction and specialised types

a thicker piece of wood, which may have been a reason for most country craftsmen's axes being without this thickened end.

Several ways of securing the handle to the axe head have been used. The simplest hole in the head is parallel in side view (Fig 2D), but elliptical in section. This gives little grip. A better shape is waisted (Fig 2E)—a shape which could be forged by a blacksmith making an individual head, and this is followed in factory manufacture today.

An axe handle is given a shoulder and the end is tapered to fit the hole in the head. Tightening is done by using the different rates of inertia of the wooden handle and the steel head. The axe is held head down in the air and the end of the handle hit with a mallet (Fig 2F). The light wood accelerates quicker than the heavy steel, so the wood enters the head. If a head loosens in use, this is the method used for tightening. Tightening can be continued until the head reaches the shoulder. At this stage a new handle has to be fitted. The end of the handle is cut to allow for hitting (Fig 2G).

Modern methods have not improved on the country craftsman's use of wedges to secure a head to a handle. Basically, a saw cut is made in the wood before the handle is fitted and a wedge driven into it to spread the wood in the waisted hole (Fig 2H). Usually the wedge is hardwood with only a slight taper, so that it penetrates deeply. One improvement was to cut the wedge with a twist so as to improve its grip. There may be a second wedge driven across the first, into a slot chopped with a chisel. Wooden wedges are satisfactory, providing they retain their grip, but it is common for the second wedge to be metal. A blacksmith formed a steel wedge with teeth chopped in its edge with a cold chisel (Fig 2J). There are modern cast wedges of similar form. Another type of smith-made wedge had its end split so that the two parts curved in opposite directions after driving.

Axes have been used by all the woodworking crafts and their

Page 33 (*top*) Staddle stones under a barn at Singleton—an early example of quantity-production; (*bottom*) local types of bill-hooks (Forestry Commission Mayswood Centre): West Country, Kent, general-purpose, Stafford, Newtown, Hampshire, Llandilo, Knighton, Leicester, Norfolk, Swindon, Bristol, Tenterden

Page 34 (top) Two carpenter's mallets, a slater's hammer, a tinman's mallet and a sheet-metalworker's bossing mallet; *(bottom)* hammers: sledge, pin, ball-pane, saddler's, prospector's, saw sharpening, Warrington and adze-eye claw

variety is accounted for by differing needs. For the maximum cut, weight is needed, but this is limited by safety factors depending on the strength of the worker. Not many centuries ago, average sizes of people were considerably smaller than today, but a man who earned his living by the strength of his arms obviously could manage tools heavier than the occasional user. A woodman using a felling axe with two hands for long periods can manage up to about 7lb head on a 36in shaft, but our lighter ancestors might have been content with about 4lb on a handle a few inches shorter. A regular user might manage a 4lb hand axe, but it would probably be safer for an occasional user to have only about half this weight to control with one hand.

The longer the handle, the greater the effectiveness of a swing, but this does not permit a very high degree of precision at the cut. Many trades used a shorter handle for greater control. In some cases, as in broom making, the head was the same as for a woodman's axe, but the haft was shortened to bring the hand close to the head. Other trades used a much wider head ('broad' axe) on a similarly shortened haft. A rake maker, and others, had a broad axe with its cutting edge twice as long as a normal axe (Fig 2K). With the hand behind the cutting edge, the action was partly slice and partly chop.

In the trades where an axe was used for trimming blocks of wood approximately to size, it was often sharpened on only one side for single-handed use (Fig 2L). This was usually called a 'side' axe. It could also be a 'broad' axe. The sharpening bevel could be either side, depending on the user being left- or right-handed. The chair bodger, preparing wood for turning chair legs and rails, used a hand axe of normal proportions, but sharpened on one side. His normally-sharpened axe for splitting from the log had a very short handle for accuracy of direction at some loss of power. The cooper's broad axe is sharpened on one side and may have a cutting edge as wide as 12in, with either a

C

straight or concave cutting edge to suit the peculiar needs of barrel-making (Fig 2M).

Some wheelwrights used an axe of fairly normal traditional appearance, except that it was sharpened on only one side and the edge was broadened towards the handle (Fig 2N). In some cases the handle was curved sideways so that the hand was out of line with the cut, allowing work to be done close to a surface without the hand interfering or touching.

Bills

For lighter chopping, particularly by the craftsmen who worked in the open, cutting wood in thickets and woods and plying their trade on the spot, there were a variety of swinging knives, akin to axes, but mostly with more blade than handle. The best-known example is the 'bill-hook (Fig 3A). Its general form has remained unchanged for centuries, but a surprising number of local preferences still persist and have to be met. While it could be argued that any one design of bill-hook should be effective at the same job in different parts of the country, factories still have to manufacture a considerable range under local names to satisfy their customers.

A similar hook on a long handle is called a 'slasher' or 'slashing hook' (Fig 3B). The long handle gives a more powerful swing and is useful for reaching a greater distance. Both hooks may be double-sided, usually with a straight knife on the back (Fig 3C). The amount of the curved point is the major difference between local bill-hooks. The tool has been called just a 'bill' or a 'bille'. Blades are not usually more than about 10in long, but all sorts of length, shape and size were produced by local craftsmen.

A bill-hook is sharpened more like a knife than an axe, with a fairly acute cutting edge, frequently touched up in use. There is no widening to give a splitting action as most cuts are light and diagonal or across the grain.

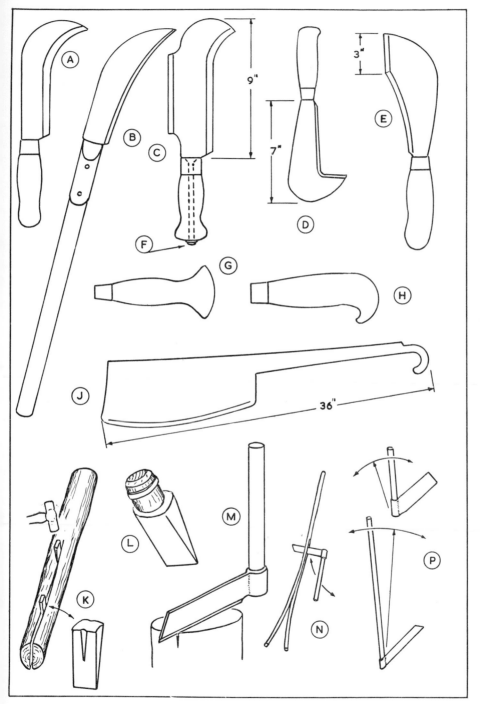

Fig 3 Chopping and splitting tools

The besom broom maker called his general-purpose tool a 'chopping bill' and had a lighter one with more curve to the point called a 'stripping bill'. Thatchers have converted bill-hooks to suit their needs by grinding off the points. Spars for thatching are made by splitting hazel and willow. For this a 'spar hook' with rather more point is favoured (Fig 3D).

A hurdlemaker used a 'trimming bill' (Fig 3E) with a straight cutting edge at the end. This functioned as a light axe for trimming inside angles of an assembled hurdle, or for finer shaping than can be done with a larger tool. The ordinary bill-hook was used for pointing palings and light fence posts, in preference to an axe.

Handles of bill-hooks are usually quite short and may vary from unshaped wood to a turned shape with a ferrule. In the best tools, a tang goes right through the handle and is riveted over a washer (Fig 3F). With the chopping action, similar to an axe, there is a tendency for the tool to fly out of the grip, so handles have been turned with enlarged ends (Fig 3G) or carved with a hook which could allow the tool to be hung up when out of use (Fig 3H).

The butcher's 'cleaver' was another form of swinging knife. The large one split carcasses and was all-steel with considerable weight (Fig 3J). A bench cleaver might have a wooden handle and be generally similar to other craftsmen's straight-bladed swinging knives.

Wedges and froes

The swinging cutting edge of an axe needs considerable skill to direct it accurately so that successive cuts fall on the same spot. The way to improve accuracy is to separate the swing from the cut—having the cutting edge in position while delivering a blow to drive it in.

Some axes have flat tops so that the axe can be held in position and hit with a mallet or hammer. This, like using the back of the axe as a hammer, is not considered good practice by British craftsmen, and it is regarded as misuse of the tool. Many American hatchets have hammer heads or pads for hitting. This probably dates from colonial pioneering days when getting as many uses as possible from a tool was an important consideration.

It could be dangerous to use a hammer on the head of a modern axe. The manufactured axe head has the same temper throughout and the face of the hammer is also hardened. One or both hard surfaces may splinter or spark, with a risk to eyes.

The simplest tool for hitting is a wedge, either steel or wood. To divide a log lengthways, a split is started with a steel wedge or the axe, then wedges driven into the split to force it along. Two, or more, wedges may be used in turn (Fig 3K). A craftsman prefers to hit wood with wood and metal with metal. So that a steel wedge could be hit with a wooden mallet or beetle, some wedges have been made with sockets to take a wooden piece, which has its top bound with steel to prevent splitting (Fig 3L).

A wedge with a handle is commonly called a 'froe' (Fig 3M), although other names are used, such as 'fromard' (probably the accepted full name, which became abbreviated to froe), 'cleaving axe', 'framod', 'doll-axe' and 'dill-axe'. Sizes are even more varied than with bill-hooks. The froe has a double purpose. It may be hit, usually with a crude cudgel, into end grain to start a split. Its sole use in this way is when short sections of log are being split into suitable pieces for chair rails or ladder rungs. For many other tasks, such as splitting hazel for dry barrel hoops, wattle hurdlemaking or for basketmaking, the froe is used to lever open and continue a split for a considerable distance (Fig 3N).

For opening a split, the froe becomes a lever rather than a cutting tool. A long handle on a comparatively narrow blade can then be seen to need less effort than a wide blade and a short handle (Fig 3P). Of course, the wider the blade within the cut, the greater the leverage and the further the splitting action. Sizes of handle and blade had to be a compromise and the best combination had to be found by trial for a particular class of work—hence the large variations between surviving froes. Wide-bladed and short-handled froes were used mainly for chopping. Long handles gave leverage for splitting and with the width of the blade this was as much as could reasonably be worked.

Adzes

An axe has its blade in line with the handle. This serves for most purposes, but there are some situations where a blade set across the line of the handle would be more use. One such situation is where the roots of a tree have to be cut off when the stump is being removed and it is more convenient to stand facing the job than across it. The tool for doing this is called a 'mattock'. It may have one blade, when it looks like a rather substantial garden hoe (Fig 4A), or be two-bladed, with the second blade in line with the handle (Fig 4B). The head may have a tapered socket to fit a handle of the pick-axe type. With these two blades it is possible to grub out roots without having to dig away too much earth. As with axes and other tools produced for local use, mattocks varied considerably in size and shape, according to local ideas. The opposite side to the mattock blade could have a split blade for cutting and removing undergrowth or weeds (Fig 4C).

A more refined tool with the blade across the line of the handle is an 'adze' (Fig 4D), which has appeared in many forms and in many trades, but basically it has a blade curved approximately to the circumference of the likely swing (Fig 4E). For work on flat surfaces it has a slight curve in its width and the sharpening is only on the upper surface (Fig 4F). An adze of this

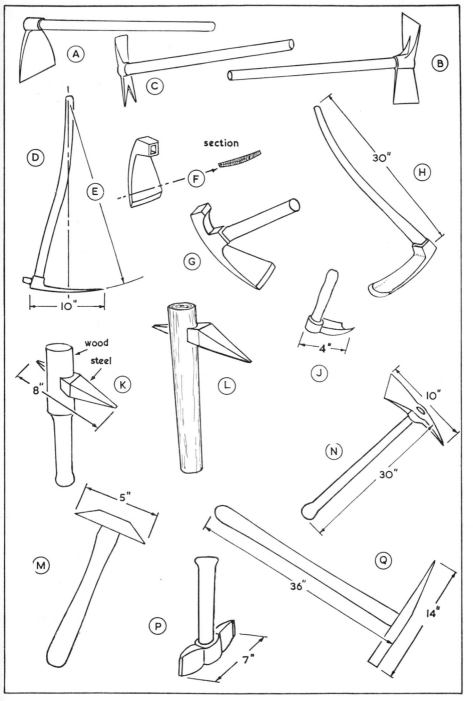

Fig 4 Adzes, mattocks and other chopping tools

type has a dog-leg haft long enough to be used while standing astride or alongside the work which is resting on the floor.

A craftsman with an adze with which he is thoroughly familiar can use it to remove anything between a shaving as fine as that from a plane and large slivers of wood. An adze skilfully used can fashion a complex shape out of a block of wood, bringing it close to the final size to be finished with other tools.

Adzes and froes may be considered tools of the past as machine tools now do some of their jobs, but there is a limited demand for them. There are still jobs for which an adze is the only satisfactory tool, and there are still particular preferences. A recent catalogue shows two types for carpenters and a London wheeler's adze, showing that locality types exist today. A heavier adze is still used by shipwrights for levelling wooden decks.

The general-purpose adze was favoured by wheelwrights. The cooper needed a short-handled one with more curve, to work inside barrels (Fig 4G). This adze, like those in some other trades, had an extension opposite the blade. While this might have some use as a hammer, it also provided balance, which was more necessary with a short handle than with one giving a longer swing.

A craftsman, known as a 'bottomer' in the chair trade, fashioned the seats of Windsor chairs, using an adze of normal size, but with more curve than usual both ways (Fig 4H), so that the tool would work the hollows of the seat.

A rather different adze was the small one, called a 'crooked axe', used for hollowing the spoons and ladles mostly made from sycamore, which were, and still are, a feature of some parts of Wales. This is a small short-handled adze with a gouge-like cross-section and a curve in the length of the blade (Fig 4J). Its shape allowed it to chop out a sufficiently-deep hollow.

Adze handles were given a dog-leg shape, such that the grip came above the point of balance in the better-designed ones.

In most cases the handle had a thickened tapered end to fit the steel socket, of such a size that the rest of the handle would pass through and the tool could be dismantled for storage.

Stone working

The 'millstone dresser', or 'mill bill', was a tool used in an axe-like manner, to cut or reshape the grooves, called 'furrows' or 'harps', in the face of the millstone. These needed to be dressed at intervals. As the stone quickly blunted the steel bill, it was usually made with a reversible and replaceable blade (Fig 4K) to reduce the number of stops needed for sharpening. The handle, sometimes called a 'thrift', was thickened wood or metal to provide weight for the blows.

A rather similar idea can be seen in a 'slater's pick' (Fig 4L), used for trimming slates, with the double-ended head slotted into a natural wood shaft. A more scientific design was the slater's trimming hammer, with cutting edges (Fig 4M) for cutting slates to shape. Masons used a number of dressing tools with an axe action. A stone chipper was something like a broad-bladed pick-axe, used with two hands (Fig 4N). For more precise work a mason used the single-handed stone-dressing hammer which was a heavy short-handled tool with cutting edges set at a fairly obtuse angle (Fig 4P). The stonemason's pick was a sort of pick-axe, but without the curve of the present-day mass-produced tool (Fig 4Q).

CHAPTER 3

Mallets and Hammers

The many types of hitting tools probably had a common origin with axes. One part of a stone in the hand might cut while another part was used for pounding. Eventually a shaft might have been attached to allow for greater power being exerted. Parallel with this development would have been the use of a log or a piece of wood for driving in stakes, or similar jobs. This would have evolved into a tool with the greater weight at the hitting end and a lighter, thinner shaft.

The early hammer and axe could have been the same tool or weapon. With the acquiring of skill and the use of other tools, rather more refined hitting tools came into being, but some quite primitive tools still have their uses. Paving stones are still levelled on their sand foundations with a piece of tree trunk on a handle.

Even the hardest woods do not have a very high relative density, so any wooden-headed hitting tool has to be bulky to deliver a sufficiently heavy blow. In some cases this is an advantage, but in many cases, something more compact is needed, so many hitting tools have heads made of steel or other metal. In general terms it has been usual to call a metal-headed hitting tool a hammer, while wooden-headed ones are mallets, although particular types have other names.

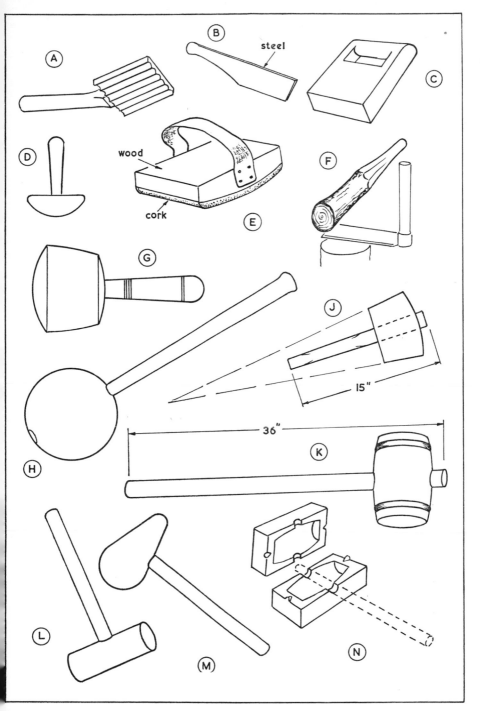

Fig 5 Mallets, beetles and other wooden hitting tools

For some woodland crafts, the tool which drives a wedge may still be just a cudgel, roughly hewn locally and used for the job in hand, then discarded. In a trade such as hurdlemaking this serves quite well, but most craftsmen in other trades moved on to something more sophisticated. Basketmakers, working in straw and withies, have mallets which are little more than cudgels. The thatcher has his 'crammer', which is merely a piece of wood, such as a barrel stave, for driving in buckles and pushing straw into place. He gives the same name to a tool like a grooved butter pat, used for 'beating up' straw thatch. For reed thatch the tool is perforated. His 'leggat' is a similar tool with its handle at an angle (Fig 5A).

Several craftsmen use almost plain blocks of wood or metal. The name 'commander' is used for this in some trades. The basketmaker uses an iron block as a beater (Fig 5B). With a handle it is a commander, although the name is also used by him for a tool for straightening stakes. The thatcher has a block of wood with a hand hole, called a spud (Fig 5C), and used for driving in pegs. Some spuds also have a tapered end to prise open gaps in the straw. The saddler uses a turned wood 'smasher' (Fig 5D). It looks like a sock darner and is used for hitting and smoothing down thread. The tanner and currier has his pommel for rubbing and hitting leather to make it supple. This is a block of wood with a shaped cork face and a strap to go around the hand (Fig 5E).

For hitting a froe or other metal tool, a simple cudgel (Fig 5F) has the advantage of being easily replaced with material to hand when it has worn out—as it would be frequently, hitting the narrow harder surface. Some workers called this a 'beetle' or 'bitel', but this name is more commonly applied to a large mallet. Another advantage of the round head is that by turning, it permits a new face to be presented to the job, so prolonging its life.

Wood carvers and stone masons have always preferred a

mallet which is a development of this cudgel type of beetle. The mallet might have been turned from one piece of wood, but more often a handle was fitted into a head (Fig 5G). For general purposes, beech was, and still is, the chosen wood, as it is dense and not easily split or broken. The turned head may be up to about 8in in diameter and 4in thick. For a more concentrated weight, and therefore a smaller or heavier head, box wood was chosen. The wood carver used a short-handled mallet. The mason favoured a similar mallet, but often with a rather longer handle. To get the required weight for driving tools into his harder material, he also used a tool of the same form, but with the head made of lead or iron, and called a 'dummy'. The butcher used a long-handled mallet to stun animals. This varied from a crude woodland tool to a turned ball head (Fig 5H). Both this and the pole axe are now illegal, having given way to more humane methods.

Beech was a wood distributed fairly evenly about Britain and carpenters' mallets seem to have been made of beech in a fairly uniform manner for a long time (Fig 5J). The striking faces slope so that, if continued, they would meet near the user's elbow, with the intention that these faces will strike squarely. The handle is also usually beech and tapered slightly for its whole length, in its depth and possibly in its width. The hand end is left angular, but the rest of the exposed handle is rounded. The handle can be driven out, but the swinging action tightens the joint. Mallet heads may be up to about 7in across.

The round form of mallet head used by many craftsmen probably developed from a section of natural tree branch or trunk. The name 'maul' has been used for some large mallets, while some craftsmen prefer 'beetle'. The public houses named 'Beetle and Wedge' indicate the once common use of the beetle for driving wedges when splitting logs. The heavy head of a beetle might have been bound to prevent splitting (Fig 5K). The cooper used a beetle of this type. While ash was the obvious choice for handle, because of its springiness and its ability to cushion some of the shock from the hands, various close-grained heavy woods were used for heads. Apple was a popular choice. In medieval agriculture crude, heavy mallets were used to break down clods of earth after ploughing.

Where the mallet has to be used on a material harder than itself, it is bound to wear. This has to be accepted if the marks which would be made by a steel hammer are to be avoided. To minimise wear, the hardest wood was chosen, and the most suitable wood generally available was box. This was used for round-headed mallets (Fig 5L), for tinsmithing, and the working of copper and precious metals. For hollowing bowls, a 'bossing mallet', turned to a pear shape (Fig 5M), was used over a hollow in the end grain of a log. A similar mallet was used for stuffing collars by a saddler, although he also used a larger, heavier, round mallet for this purpose.

When a round mallet head is made from a complete section of log it is less likely to split than if turned from part of a log, as its annual rings follow completely around the head. Handles were usually round and wedged into a parallel hole.

For some purposes, such as hitting the softer metals to shape or stretch them, a wooden mallet might be too hard and leather mallets were made. Rawhide was rolled into a cylinder, sealed with glue and held to shape with nails. This was bored and a handle fitted so that the finished tool looked like a wooden mallet. Leather does not provide much weight in itself—a head about 4in long and 2½in in diameter weighs about 1lb. For some jobs needing gentle blows this was satisfactory, but if more weight were needed, sheet lead was rolled inside the leather.

Copper and lead heads were made for jobs requiring a more concentrated blow with a face that would not damage iron or steel. As lead melts at a comparatively low temperature, it

48

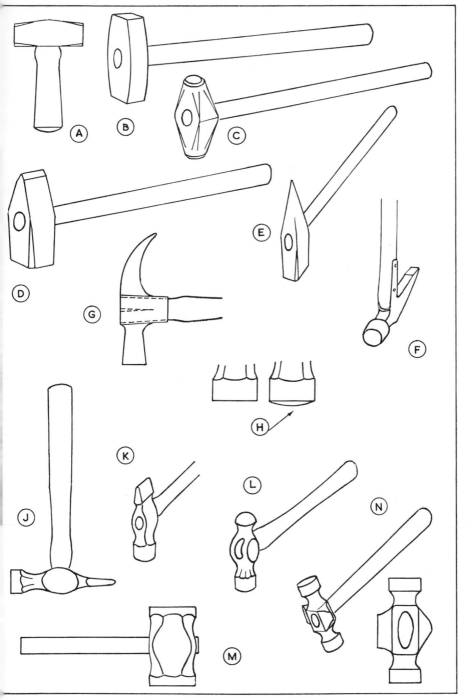

Fig 6 Special hammers and combination hitting tools

could be melted in a pot over a smithy fire. A mould would be kept to cast lead hammer heads from scrap. With a two-part iron mould which had a hole to take a steel rod handle, the head could be cast on the handle (Fig 5N). Thus, a battered lead mallet could soon be melted and remade on the same handle.

There is still a need for soft-faced mallets or hammers, but today steel heads with inset faces of copper, lead, rawhide, rubber or other materials are available. There are also plastic-faced hammers in which the plastic parts are easily changed.

A mallet may be said to deliver a 'soft' blow as there is not the rebound or spring that goes with the steel head of a hammer. A mallet is useful for driving parts together, whereas a hammer is more suitable on a cold chisel, a spike or other object needing a concentrated blow. A mallet is also used on softer materials so that they are not damaged. A woodworking craftsman has always used a mallet on the wooden handle of a chisel but, with the coming of plastic handles there seems to be no reason, except tradition, for him not to use a hammer on the tougher material.

Hammers

The basic hammer was a piece of steel or other metal, probably square, with a handle fitted through a hole. There are hammer heads of iron and bronze, dating from prehistoric days, still in existence, with forms much the same as hammers used by some craftsmen today. The stone mason still uses hammers near to this basic form. His 'club' or 'mash' hammer concentrates weight into a squarish head, weighing up to 4lb and mounted on a short ash handle (Fig 6A). This is his general purpose single-handed hammer, used mostly for hitting other tools. Stone workers used a variety of two-handed hammers. The origin of 'sledge' as the name for a two-handed hammer is unknown, but it is commonly used in several trades. A mason's

Page 51 (top) A slasher and a maul or beetle; (bottom) chisels and their handles: a socket-handled gouge, a heavy-duty chisel with a bound handle, a mortice chisel, an unhandled chisel showing its tang, a firmer chisel, a paring chisel with octagonal handle, three carving tools

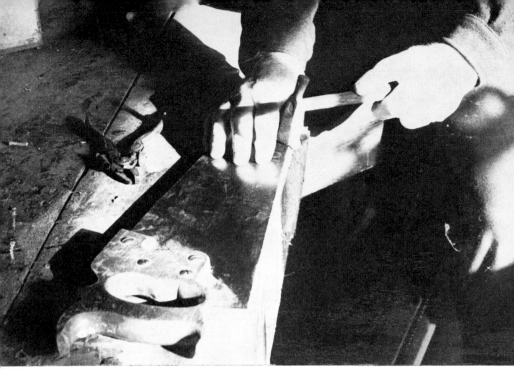

Page 52 (*top*) Setting saw teeth with a hammer over the end of an iron block. A plier saw set is on the bench; (*bottom*) model of a Chinese rip saw, at the home of George Bernard Shaw, Ayot St Lawrence

'spalling' hammer is large and heavy, with rectangular faces (Fig 6B). A stone breaking hammer is similar, but with a shaping towards rounded faces (Fig 6C). A stone waller has a sledge hammer with one straight pane, sharpened for squaring or cutting stones or bricks roughly to shape (Fig 6D). The same sort of hammer with a point instead of a straight pane is called a 'scabbling' hammer (Fig 6E) and is used for roughly dressing stone.

The hammer suffers from the same problem as an axe, with centrifugal force tending to make a loose head fly off in use. Most hammer heads were, and still are, fitted to their handles by being driven through a waisted hole then spread with one or more wedges, as described for axes. For extra strength there could be tangs forged on each side of the head, to allow rivets through the handle (Fig 6F). A firmer grip can be obtained by having a deeper 'adze eye' (Fig 6G), but hammers of this type are more the product of industry than of rural craftsmen, who would have used the waisted elliptical eye for locally made hammers.

A few native craftsmen in the East use hammers with heads at one side of the handle only, but in most parts of the world the head crosses the handle and has two faces, or 'panes' ('pein' and other spellings). This provides better balance and allows different purposes for the two faces, if desired. For most trades, the normal hitting face is round and does not project very far from the handle. Some craftsmen favour a slight curve to the face (Fig 6H). In skilled hands this is not so likely to mark a surface as a flat face. A cabinetmaker claims to be able to drive a nail or pin flush with a curved-pane hammer without bruising the surrounding wood. The other face could be the same, but in most cases it has another purpose. What may be considered the modern general purpose equivalent of hammers traditionally used in many rural crafts is now known as the Warrington-pattern hammer (Fig 6J). For general woodworking this may be anything between 6oz and 25oz. The smith has a basically similar, much heavier hammer.

The narrow cross-pane gets into restricted places, starts nails held between the fingers and is used for rivetting. Less common, but used by blacksmiths and engineers, is a straight-pane, in line with the handle (Fig 6K).

If a straight or cross pane is brought down on hot or soft metal, the metal is thinned and spread in a direction at right-angles to the line of the pane. If the spread is required in all directions, the hammer is given a ball-pane (Fig 6L). This is useful in closing rivets, although the initial spreading is often done with a straight-pane. Nowadays the Warrington-pattern is the general-purpose hammer for the woodworker and the ball-pane for the metalworker.

In chair making, where a great many joints had to be driven progressively, a short-handled hammer of almost mallet proportions was used to give the short, but weighty, blows needed to draw all the parts together (Fig 6M).

The farrier used a number of hammers for horse shoeing. The catshead hammer (Fig 6N) was quite a heavy hammer with two almost similar faces, but one flat and one convex, and with projections at the sides, used for forming the clip on the front of a shoe. There were other hammers of more straight-forward design, up to 3lb for cart horse shoes, about $2\frac{1}{2}$lb for lighter work, and a hammer under 14oz with a face the size of a 5p piece for nailing on.

Although claw hammers were not in very common use by country craftsmen, their use for withdrawing nails was known from early days and the farrier might include one in his kit, which was traditionally housed in a tapered open-topped box. A claw hammer head, looking very much like its modern equivalent, has been found and identified as dating from the second century (Fig 7A).

Another user of a claw hammer was the slater, who may have

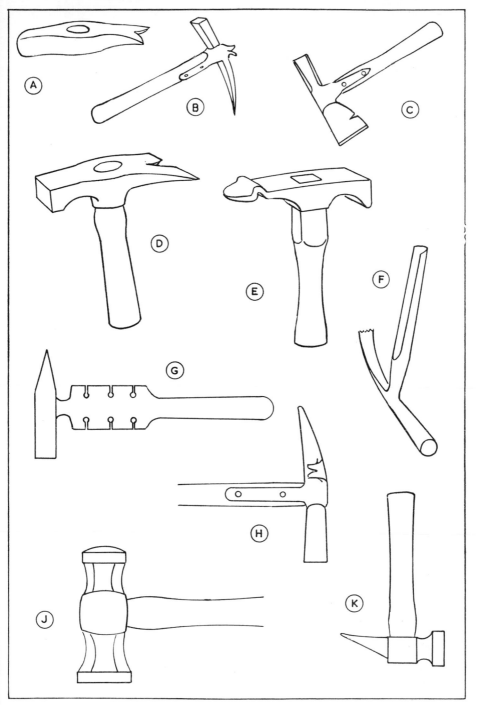

Fig 7 Hammers for various purposes

been supporting himself precariously on a roof and was glad of a combination tool which avoided changing or dropping tools. The slater also had a 'pick hammer' (Fig 7B). Its flat face would drive nails or pegs, the pick end would strike holes in slates or woodwork, and the claw on the side would withdraw nails. Another of his combination tools was his 'lath hatchet' (Fig 7C), used when fixing the laths to rafters to support the slates or tiles. The hatchet side cut the laths to length. The flat face drove nails, and there was usually a notch in the side of the hatchet to withdraw nails.

A cooper's nailing adze, despite its name, was a hammer used mostly for repairing or replacing wooden hoops (Fig 7D). The tapered side could be used for levering. It might have a straight chisel edge or be notched for withdrawing fastenings. A rather similar hammer from Denmark was a 'butter firkin' hammer (Fig 7E), used for opening and closing a butter cask. The cranked piece gave extra leverage when the thin end was used to lever off a top. A cheese taster with a hammer head (Fig 7F) was another combination tool from the dairy.

For saw sharpening, a light hammer was used for setting alternate teeth by hitting them over the bevelled edge of an anvil before filing to sharpen them. For the finer teeth this would be done by a very thin cross-pane. For large teeth, as found in cross-cut and pit saws, a notched steel plate was used for setting alternate teeth by hitting them over the bevelled edge of an anvil before filing to sharpen them. For the finer teeth this would be done by a very thin cross-pane. For large teeth, as found in cross-cut and pit saws, a notched steel plate was used to lever the teeth each way. There are specimens where the saw set and hammer were incorporated in the same tool (Fig 7G).

Workers in leather or fabric were mostly concerned with driving tacks or pins, so the hammer could be light. Saddlers and upholsterers had light, graceful hammers, with the driving side of the head quite long and thin. This was balanced by a tapered side, which might go to a point or be rounded (Fig 7H). Because of the small section making the usual oval eye too small to give a secure attachment to the handle, these hammers had tangs forged on each side. There could be a nail claw on the side. A similar light hammer was used by the clogmaker, for tacking uppers to the wooden sole, but the bootmaker needed a heavier hammer with a broad face for dressing leather over a last. This might have been double-faced, with one side flat and the other convex (Fig 7J). A similar hammer, possibly rather lighter, has one side tapered to a cross-pane (Fig 7K) and is nowadays called a 'shoe hammer'.

CHAPTER 4

Knives

At least one knife appears amongst the equipment of all who work in fabric, leather, wood and any material soft enough to be cut with this tool. For some crafts, a knife is almost the only tool. In more primitive circumstances in the past, and amongst some primitive peoples today, the knife is depended on as a weapon, tool and eating implement. From the sharp flint, which may have been more of a scraper than a knife, progress was made through the early metals until steel was developed. Steel, in much the same form, has been the material for knives and other cutting tools for many centuries. The only recent developments have been the addition of small quantities of other elements to give special qualities to the blade, such as the ability to retain an edge longer or to give resistance to corrosion.

The primary use of early knives would have been as daggers, so a sharp point was of more use than cutting edges. For craft work a side cutting edge was more important, although a point would have been useful for making holes. Cutting edges on both sides might have been found on a dagger, but would be of doubtful advantage for working, apart from giving extra cutting surface and therefore delaying the need to sharpen. For many jobs this would be outweighed by danger and the un-

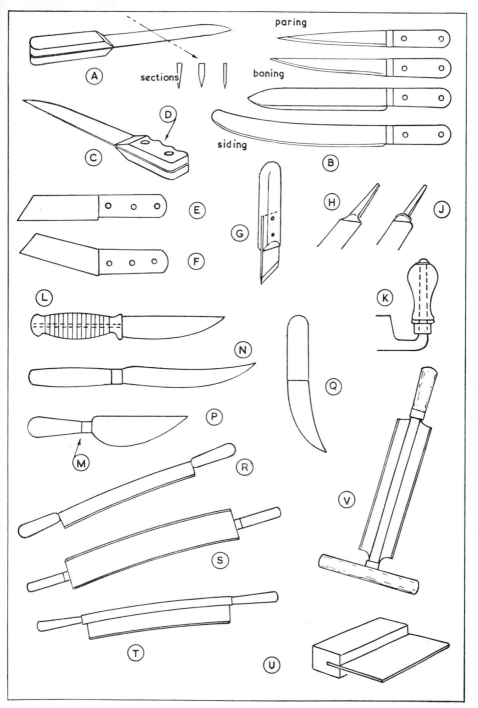

Fig 8 Knives for general use or special purposes

suitability for putting pressure directly over the cutting edge with the other hand.

The basic knife, on which there seem to be an infinite number of variations, has a handle long enough to grip with one hand and a blade either parallel in its thickness or of a wedge section; usually straight, but with the cutting edge and the back curved to meet in a point (Fig 8A).

Early knives possibly had handles made by binding leather around an extended piece from the blade, a simple way out of the difficulty of drilling or forming steel with the tools available. However, if holes could be drilled or punched by the smith during manufacture, a handle could be made by riveting pieces each side. General-purpose knives for many trades still have this type of handle. In particular, most of the knives favoured by the butcher have riveted handles (Fig 8B).

Parallel pieces of hardwood are usual (Fig 8C). There may be finger grooves to give a safer grip (Fig 8D). Other materials than wood may have been used, but bone and similar materials would have been chosen for decorative reasons, although horns and antlers provided ready-bored handles for some knives. Leather riveted each side may not have given as comfortable a grip, but this is still found in some glaziers' knives. Their 'hacking' (Fig 8E) and 'chipping' knives (Fig 8F) have leather handles and blades with thick backs so that they will withstand hammering as they are used for removing old glass and putty.

Instead of taking the blade right through, it was sometimes let only a short distance into a solid handle and riveted. This allows a more comfortable grip to be fashioned as well as reducing the amount of steel needed. It particularly suits short-bladed knives, such as the marking knife (Fig 8G) used by cabinetmakers, wheelwrights and other precision woodworkers. Today this knife is giving way to the mass-produced trimming knife with a replaceable blade.

Many knives had a tang forged by the smith, probably with a squared taper, to drive into a handle—usually plain (Fig 8H), although a shoulder (Fig 8J) made a neater job. The shoulder was an advantage if the main use of the knife was a pushing action. Where the action tended to pull the handle from the blade, as in a draw knife, the tang would be almost parallel and long enough to be taken through and riveted (Fig 8K).

A type of handle used in American hunting knives, but less common elsewhere, has a series of washerlike pieces threaded on the tang and shaped to make a comfortable grip. The pieces may be leather, or plastic today, with metal ends (Fig 8L).

While turned handles are acceptable for draw and other two-handed knives, a flat or elliptical section is better for a single-handed knife as it ensures a directional grip. For blades fitted with a tang, a brass or other tubular metal ferrule is advisable to prevent splitting of the wood (Fig 8M). The seating for this might have been turned, but the handle would be carved or whittled for a normal knife, giving the worker an opportunity for some artistic expression. An example of this type is the basketmaker's general-purpose pointed 'shop knife' (Fig 8N). Very similar is his 'picking knife' (Fig 8P), with a broad curved cutting edge, for trimming finished baskets.

Pocket knives of the clasp or folding type have been more a product of industry than of country craftsmen, although there are examples of knives made by individual craftsmen in which the blade folds or withdraws into the handle. Despite local prejudices and the preferences of craftsmen in various trades for knives of particular patterns, the availability of cheap government surplus army clasp knives after World War I has brought an acceptance of this as a satisfactory alternative to a large variety of knives previously traditionally used.

While most craftsmen have a general-purpose knife in their kit, workers in leather need a large variety. The tanner had one or more large knives of the butcher type and one with a hooked blade, similar to that used today for cutting floor covering (Fig 8Q). He used a two-handed knife with a pushing action for removing hair on a hanging skin (Fig 8R). After further treatment of the skin a 'fleshing knife', which had a slight curve in side view, was used (Fig 8S). The concave edge scraped while the convex edge cut. For a further process, a similar, one-sided 'scudder knife' (Fig 8T) had a stiffened back between the handles.

A currier followed the tanner, softening and preparing the leather for use. He used a 'sleaker' for forcing out dirt (Fig 8U). This did not cut, but was used with pressure from both hands all over the surface of the leather. The currier also had an unusual knife for scraping skins: a wide two-edge blade was stiffened along its centre with a straight handle at one end and another across at the other end (Fig 8V). The knife is sharpened, then held by the straight handle between the knees with the other handle on the ground, and then the cutting edges are turned over to about right-angles by rubbing a piece of hard steel many times, with plenty of pressure along the edge. This produces an edge something like a cabinetmaker's scraper. The turned-over edge is then used to scrape a thin layer off the flesh side of the leather before treating it with oil.

A saddler uses a large number of knives in various sizes. Some of them are basic, but a number are peculiar to his needs. Current usage is not so very different from that of many centuries and knives of traditional type are still in production. A short-bladed knife, with its blade at an angle, is used for thinning and paring edges of leather. There was also an edge trimmer or 'skirt shave' (Fig 9A), something like a wood chisel but with solid sides, used for bevelling the edge of a saddle skirt and between $\frac{1}{2}$in and $\frac{3}{4}$in wide. The farrier's 'buttress knife' was a rather similar tool, cutting on the end, but with turned-up 'safe' edges (Fig 9B) or a gouge section. This was used for

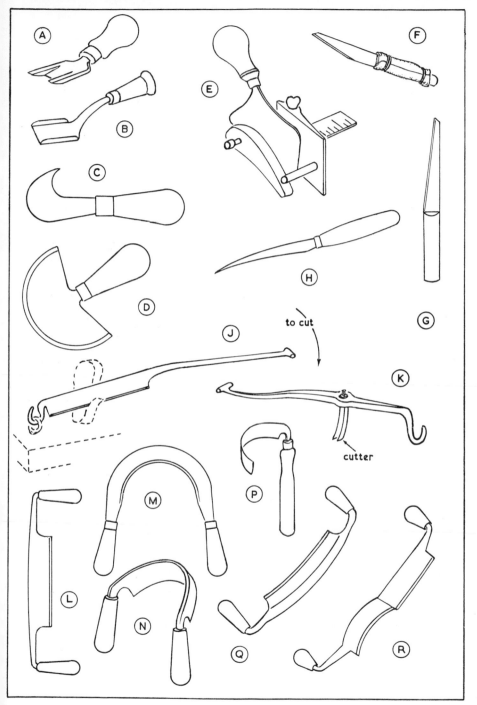

Fig 9 Special knives and variations on the draw knife

scooping out the sole of a hoof and might be about 14in long so that the handle could be pushed from under the armpit.

Holes and other internal curves in leather are cut with a 'head knife', having a hooked end rather similar to the tanner's hooked knife (Fig 9C). The saddler's 'half moon knife' is peculiar to the trade (Fig 9D). It is a general-purpose knife, up to 7in across, which can be used with a slicing or rocking motion.

A knife blade mounted so that a stop controlled the width being cut was used for straps and similar parallel leather pieces. This developed into the leather plough (Fig 9E), still in use.

The village bootmaker had a large array of knives amongst which was a paring knife, going back to first principles, being a plain piece of steel, around which went a wrapped leather handle (Fig 9F). He also used a hooked knife, similar to that of the saddler, but more likely called a 'hawk bill'. A knife with a sloping edge, like the saddler's paring knife, was called a 'clip point'. With a wooden handle (Fig 9G) it served for many purposes, including cutting uppers, while a similar knife with a longer and more flexible blade was used for heels. A more delicate knife was called a 'stitcher' and used for cutting threads. A 'clicker' (Fig 9H) was a knife with a fine blade, used for cutting leather to shape; its name coming from the noise it makes when being drawn around templates.

The clogmaker used most of the bootmaker's tools, but needed special equipment for the soles. Making clog soles might have been done by itinerant workers or by a village craftsman who combined the work with bootmaking. In Britain, clogs always had leather uppers and were never of the completely wooden type used in Holland and other parts of the continent. Many woods were used, but sycamore was most popular for the better clogs, although much alder was used. These are fairly hard, close-grained woods, needing more pressure to cut than could be exerted with a knife held in the hand.

To make clog soles, felled wood was cut up while still green;

no time being allowed for seasoning. First cuts were by beetle and wedge, followed by a side axe, then the clogger tackled these billets of wood with his 'stock knife' (Fig 9J). This might be up to 30in long to give leverage, with the blade about half this and the hooked end fitting quite loosely into a large staple or ring on a rigidly-supported bench top, arranged so that the handle overhangs. The clogmaker operated the knife with one hand while manipulating the sole with the other. By moving the sole about and turning the knife in its staple, the required outline could be obtained by a combination of slicing and chopping. The roughly-shaped sole was left to season before finishing. A rakemaker used a similar tool, called a 'peg knife', for levelling and pointing wooden rake teeth.

A knife of similar general form, but with a convex blade, was used for hollowing the top surface of a clog to the foot shape. The upper was nailed around the side of the sole, but a channel had to be worked to take the edge of the leather. A gougelike blade in an iron arm, called a 'morticing knife', was operated in the same way as a stock knife to do this (Fig 9K).

Draw knives

A widely used tool amongst rural craftsmen was the draw knife. There were many variations in design, but the use of two hands to pull a knife over a piece of wood which was fixed down allowed for the application of considerable skill, so that the finish was acceptable in many cases, without further treatment. The blade could be sharpened on both sides, but if sharpened on one side and used bevel-downwards, altering the angle of pull on the handles could cause variations in the cut to produce anything from fine shavings to large chips, or allow for working into hollows. Much of the decorative notching and bevelling on waggons was done entirely by work with the draw knife, mainly as light finishing touches after the heavy work of building the waggon was finished.

The draw knife basic to many trades was straight and flat in section and with a cutting edge a foot or so long. The handles might have been plain pieces of wood or, preferably, turned handles with bulbous ends, to prevent pulling through the hand and tangs taken through and rivetted over a washer (Fig 9L). Such a knife was used for roughing wood to shape for chair leg bodging, shaping spales for basketmaking, making broom handles, forming rake parts, hurdlemaking, preparing strips for coracle making and also in waggon and wheel making.

The basic draw knife may have had a first use in removing bark, but the wooden rake maker and others used a curved cutting tool. This draw shave worked on the same principle, but the blade has considerable curve and the tangs go straight from the ends of the blade into the handles (Fig 9M). For rounding spars, such as are used for brush handles, a draw knife with considerable curve in the width gets a better finish quickly, so the broom squire, who made besoms, used a light round shave (Fig 9N).

The cooper has the greatest need for a variety of draw knives. Besides one of basic pattern, he uses a round shave, similar to that used for broom handle making, but shaped and sharpened for paring inside barrel staves. Beside the two-handled type, a single-handed version allows access to more inaccessible places (Fig 9P). For the first hollowing of staves a draw knife with a moderate curve in its width, called a 'hollowing knife', was used (Fig 9Q).

Other coopers' draw knives had special names, but not all the same in different areas. A 'heading' or 'backing' knife was a draw knife with a concave curve in side view, used for making the bevelled edge round the head (flat end) of a barrel or cask. A 'jigger' was a draw knife with a partly straight and partly hollowed blade (Fig 9R). A Runcorn jigger was a draw knife with a narrow convex blade and long handles.

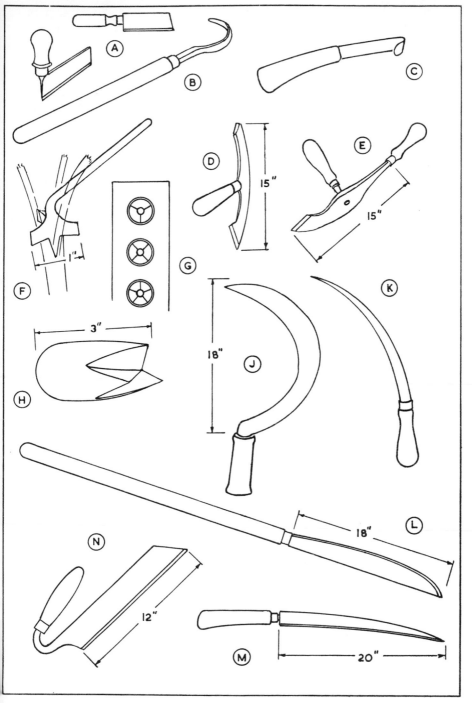

Fig 10 Knives and splitters for coppice and straw crafts

Special shaped knives

While the froe and beetle were needed for splitting fairly substantial lengths of wood, some country craftsmen doing lighter work such as trug basketmaking used a 'cleaver', something between a one-handled draw knife and a small froe, which could be pressed through or hit with a mallet or hammer (Fig 10A).

Wooden spoon makers (an especially Welsh craft) worked mostly in sycamore and needed tools more delicate than in most other crafts. Outside curves were finished by whittling with an ordinary knife, but the hollow of the spoon would be roughed to shape with the small adze, called a 'crooked axe' (Fig 4J), followed by a 'crooked knife' (Fig 10B). The light, curved blade was in a handle long enough to go under one arm while the other hand manipulated the blade to pare the inside of the spoon. Similar hooked knives, with short handles and sharpened inside for pulling, were used by several other craftsmen for light trimming. Another variation was the farrier's hoof cleaning knife (Fig 10C). The bootmaker used a similar knife, with a wider cut, for paring with a pull stroke; the same form is seen in a version of the woodman's scribing knife, used for marking letters and numbers on felled timber.

A gate (also spelled 'gait') hurdle is mortice and tenonned together. Traditionally the tenons were shaped with an axe, bill-hook or draw knife, but the mortice had their ends drilled and the waste removed with a special mortice knife (Fig 10D). The knife-edged end chops the waste wood from between the holes and the opposite end digs it out. Hurdles were traditionally made from willow, which is very soft. If the method were attempted in harder woods there would be splitting. The mortice knife had a variety of local names: 'Twobill', 'twibill', 'twivel', 'dader' and 'tomahawk'. A variation had two handles and was used with a push instead of a swing, giving better directional control (Fig 10E).

Straw was plaited for the making of hats. While some plaiting was done with whole straws, finer work was done with split straws, sometimes called 'skeing'. Although splitting could be done with an ordinary knife, special 'straw splitters' were introduced at the beginning of the nineteenth century. With a short handle, various numbers of blades could be mounted at equal spacings to split straws (Fig 10F). Later, similar cutter arrangements were mounted in a block of wood, each hole having blades to divide the straw differently (Fig 10G).

The same principle in a larger tool was found in the basketmaker's 'cleaver' (Fig 10H). Withy (willow) rods were mostly used in the full round, but could be divided into three or four with these tools. The besom broom squire also used one of these cleavers to split willow for binding broom heads. A cleaver might have been made of a close-grained wood, such as holly or box, or it could have been bone and might have steel cutting edges. Splits were started in the end of the rod, then the cleaver pushed along, so that its progress was a wedge action rather than a cut.

The thatcher uses many knives. From the nature of his material it is understandable that many of these bear a family resemblance to those used, or once used, for harvesting. A 'shearing hook' (Fig 10J) for trimming thatch, is very similar to a sickle. With rather less curve it is called an 'eaves hook' (Fig 10K). An eaves or paring knife has a long handle and a long blade (Fig 10L). This is used for reaching and trimming the straw or reed at the eaves. A similar blade, but on a short handle, is used for trimming at the apex of the roof (Fig 10M). As thatchers' knives were often made by their users from old sickle blades and similar things, there were many variations in design and arrangement of handles. Having the handle turned back gave clearance for deeper cuts (Fig 10N).

The farmer and rick thatcher had a use for a very large knife on a long handle for cutting closely-packed stacked hay (Fig

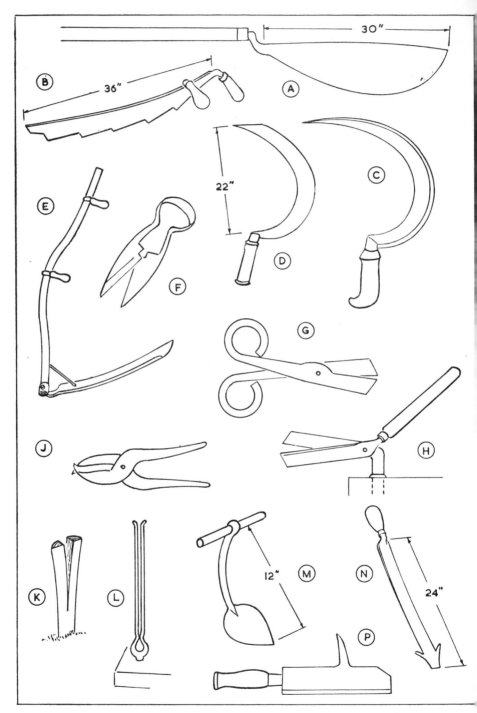

Fig 11 Cutting tools for agriculture, shears and slaters' tools

11A). As an aid to cutting, a variation had a serrated cutting edge, to give an effect something like a saw (Fig 11B), and two hand grips.

Sickles

Before the coming of machinery for reaping and grass cutting the work had to be done by hand using various sorts of swinging curved knives having a variety of names, but conveniently collectively called 'sickles'.

The basic reaping hook had considerable curve and a handle either straight out of one side (Fig 11C) or cranked slightly to give clearance on the ground. Sharpening is on the inside of the curve and on both sides of the metal. To do the job properly the edge has to be quite fine, so frequent sharpening is necessary. The user carried his sharpening stone in a sheath on his belt. This sickle may be called a 'trimmer' in America. An Austrian version has grooves towards the edge on one side, so that as the tool is sharpened a fine, sawlike serrated edge is made, providing a grip on the grass being cut as the tool is swept across it.

The hook used for grass cutting was pointed and had quite a light section so that the weight was slight. For cutting stouter weeds and light undergrowth the tool was thicker and had more weight towards the point. This might be called a 'bagging', 'fagging' or 'fag' hook (Fig 11D).

These tools were single-handed and must have been backaching to use for long periods. The tool for use standing more upright and with two hands is a 'scythe'. Blades were anything between 18in (for restricted places) and 38in (for open fields) long, with a more moderate curve than a sickle, but with more width in the blade and a fairly thick back to give stiffness. A finely-sharpened edge had to be maintained and frequent sharpening was necessary.

The scythe handle is called a 'sneathe' in a recent catalogue.

but this name, of old English origin, is also spelled 'snaith', 'snedd' or 'snath' (America). There are two handles on the sneathe and it is their position in relation to the blade which is vital, so that the shape of the sneathe is not important providing it has the handles correctly located. This is seen in wide variations in sneathe shape. In the southern half of England there is a considerable double curvature (Fig 11E) and it is this shape which is best known in illustrations. In the north of Britain the curves are very much less pronounced, although no British scythe sneathes are straight. On the Continent of Europe scythe makers get their handles in the correct place by using a straight sneathe.

Scythe sneathes are usually made of ash. The handles have been called 'doles'. Their position on the sneathe can be altered and the blade can be removed. A worker may have several blades of different sizes. Nowadays the fittings for holding the blade and handles may have a screw action for locking, but older scythes had the doles with iron rings fitting loosely on the sneathe, to which they were locked by wedging. Scythe blades have a hook end. This was also wedged into an iron fitting on the end of the sneathe. Larger blades had a small strut to a point higher on the sneathe to assist rigidity.

The best position for the doles to suit a particular worker would be found by experiment, although it was said that if the scythe was stood blade up, one dole should be at hip level and the other at a distance from it equal to the distance from elbow to fist.

Shears

The scissor or shear action of two crossing cutters seems to have been an early discovery, for there are Iron Age remains of tools using the principle. Sheep shears (Fig 11F), with a springy top, were used by thatchers and others for trimming straw and similar jobs besides shearing sheep. Conventional scissors were made in many sizes. Early examples of smaller ones, used for tailoring and dressmaking, were very similar to those used today. The brushmaker had larger ones, like garden shears, but with eye handles (Fig 11G) for hand use and another pair with an arm to fit a socket for bench use (Fig 11H).

For greater leverage, tools similar to modern tinsnips had long handles and short blades. Modern pruning shears are a development of shears used by basketmakers (Fig 11J). Tools of the tinsnips type, with straight or eye handles, were used for sheet metalwork at least as far back as the Middle Ages. The metalworker's bench shears, for stouter metal, with a long handle and a toggle action to give more leverage, seem to have been more of a product of the Industrial Revolution.

Strippers

In woodland crafts, much stripping of bark was done by draw knife and axe. Where bark would come away easily, as with newly-cut green willow, it was started with a knife, then peeled off by pulling through a split board (Fig 11K) or an iron 'peeling brake' (Fig 11L).

With most woods the bark was discarded, but oak bark was removed in large pieces and used for tanning leather. The woodman's 'barking iron' for stripping oak bark had a pointed spade blade and a cross handle for two-handed pushing and levering (Fig 11M).

The slater still uses a 'ripper' (Fig 11N) for getting under slates to cut off nails by jerking one of the notches against them and allowing the slate to be removed. He also has a 'sax' for trimming slates to size and for picking holes for nails (Fig 11P). The name 'sax', or 'zax', is an interesting example of the continued use of an old English word for knife.

CHAPTER 5

Chisels

There would have been little to choose between the earliest knives, chisels and scrapers, as they were combined in sharpened flints and other stones. Examples in many museums, dating from many thousands of years BC, are of handles made of horn, and of flints sharpened to a gouge section. Bronze Age tools followed, employing the first use of a socket, cast in the tool to take a handle. Wrought iron tools generally similar to those used today dating from the Roman occupation of Britain have been found, even bevel-edged chisels (Fig 12A).

For many woodland crafts, axe and draw knife have provided sufficient precision for the job in hand. A hurdle, rake or basket is just as satisfactory if a dimension is an inch or so different from what was intended. The maker of furniture, wheels, carts and other more exact wooden items had to be more precise, and may have had to cut accurate joints. In all but the crudest outdoor carpentry, quite a high degree of precision is needed. Even if the medieval craftsmen did not attempt close-fitting drawers and other accurate woodwork of more recent cabinet-makers, he still needed to fit parts accurately—doors must close and spokes must fit. For all of these jobs a variety of chisels and related tools are needed. Even today, with considerable mechanisation, a craftsman needs a large range of chisels.

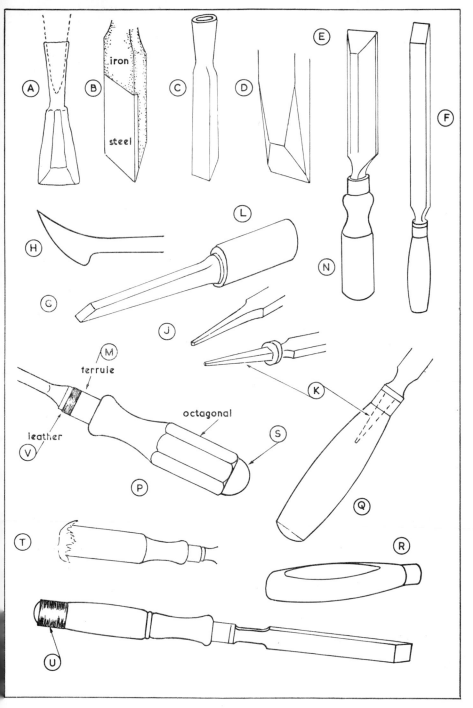

Fig 12 Chisels and chisel handles

Iron is too soft to retain a good cutting edge, and sharp tools only became possible with the coming of steel. In the Middle Ages steel was not plentiful and was costly. Because of this, and also because steel was not as malleable as iron so could not be worked as easily, chisels and other cutting tools were made by the smith welding thin steel to iron. This could be hardened, tempered and sharpened, but the body of the tool was softer iron (Fig 12B). Some plane 'irons' are still made this way, but modern chisels and other edge tools are nearly all made of steel throughout.

There might seem no logical reason why a chisel should not be made entirely of metal and hit with a hammer, but even from early days, a wooden handle has been favoured, to give a good grip. As the end of this would soon suffer if regularly hit with a hammer, it has always been customary to use a wooden mallet when a chisel has to be hit.

Metal driven into wood may split it, so if the wood can be fitted into the metal, a tool is produced which is likely to stand up better to heavy hammering. Probably because of this, many early chisels were of the socket type; the smith being able to forge a socket into which a tapered wooden handle could be fitted. The basic wood chisel then had a blade of rectangular section (Fig 12C), usually wider at the cutting edge. Parallel sides are more a product of the modern machine edge. Widths were as needed, but could be anywhere between $\frac{3}{16}$in and 2in for general woodwork. The shipwright used one nearer 3in wide with a curved blade, and called it a 'slice', for paring the slots in pulley blocks.

The general-purpose chisel is now called a 'firmer' chisel, which seems to be a corruption of the earlier name of 'forming' chisel. Corners might be ground off to allow for getting into acute angles (Fig 12D). Modern chisels may be bought already fully bevel-edged (Fig 12E). Two variations on the basic chisel were, and still are, found. A longer and thinner chisel for hand pressure only was called a 'paring' or 'heading' chisel (Fig 12F). For heavy hitting, as when chopping out hard wood, the chisel was made thicker and is now called a 'mortice' chisel (Fig 12G). For fitting door locks within the thickness of the wood, a deep mortice had to be chopped. To facilitate getting the chips from the bottom a hook-shaped 'lock mortice chisel' was used (Fig 12H).

Socket chisels had a handle made from any close-grained hardwood. Timber from fruit trees was popular, and beech was commonly used. The best handles were turned, but many were roughly whittled, and probably frequently replaced. If a chisel is given a tang to fit into a handle, such an arrangement is only suitable for use with light hand pressure (Fig 12J), unless a shoulder is also provided (Fig 12K). This is usual today, but regular shouldering does not appear to date from much before the Industrial Revolution.

If the handle were quite thick, there would not be much risk of the tang splitting it. Large oval handles were used for mortice and other heavily-used chisels (Fig 12L). For a more slender handle, there had to be a metal ferrule to prevent splitting (Fig 12M). Turned handles were made from various woods, including ash, beech and box, with a length of brass tube used as a ferrule. Shapes would depend on the skill of the local turner, but they were fashioned to give a good hand grip and stand up to hitting on the end. Shapes which have continued today have a parallel part, then shaping behind the ferrule (Fig 12N), a similar shape with the parallel part octagonal (Fig 12P), and a barrel shape (Fig 12Q). For narrow chisels the round handle might have a flat planed on it to prevent rolling (Fig 12R). Chisels wider than the handle would resist rolling in any case. By giving the end of the handle a domed or rounded top (Fig 12S), any tendency to burr over (Fig 12T) or split when hit was delayed. If the handle were intended to be hit with a hammer, as with some masons'

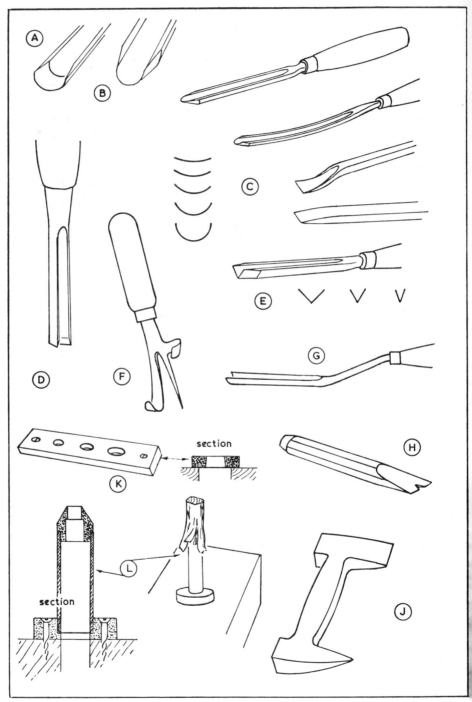

Fig 13 Gouges, carving tools and special cutters

chisels, there was a ferrule at the top as well (Fig 12U). Modern catalogues describe this as a 'registered' chisel. Of course, modern plastic handles stand up to hitting with a hammer.

A leather washer was sometimes fitted between the shoulder and the handle (Fig 12V). Some modern sash mortice chisels have this to cushion the shock of hitting.

Parallel with the development of chisels was the gouge, which is merely a chisel with a curved cross-section. Gouges are not as frequently needed as chisels, but there have been gouges made in all the forms that have been available in chisels, including light paring gouges and heavy socketed ones for hollowing work. For paring to a curve that matches the outside of the gouge, it has to be sharpened inside and this is called 'in-cannelled' (Fig 13A). For gouging out a hollow, the tool is used to lever out chips and for this it is sharpened outside, called 'out-cannelled' (Fig 13B). For deep hollowing the cutting edge may be rounded, but for general use it is straight across. Turning gouges also have rounded edges (Fig 29L). The primitive gouges, used for hollowing out tree trunks, could be regarded as the ancestors of the adze as much as of the present-day gouge.

Until a century or so ago, wood carving would not have been regarded by many as an exclusive craft. Many craftsmen in wood would have exercised their artistic ability decorating their work with carving or merely fashioning something for its own aesthetic sake. Exceptions were those engaged in church building, where the artist in stone might also work in wood or have a companion doing this. Most of these specialist craftsmen were monks rather than rural craftsmen.

The wheelwright had his edge bevelling. Many old boxes and chests have carving, ranging from geometric patterns to low relief figures, depending on the artistic ability of the man who made the article. Helical patterns were worked around tool shafts. An animal might be carved on the end of a handle.

These things would have been done with the tools of the basic trade.

As carving became more of a craft in itself, special tools developed. Carved work was particularly popular during much of the nineteenth century and almost every piece of woodwork was expected to have something carved on it. Specialist carving tended to become very ornate and this involved having a large variety of tools, mostly gouges. Gouges were made in many widths and with cross-sections, or 'sweeps', ranging from almost flat to quite deep curves. Additionally, most of these were also available cranked or otherwise shaped. Together with a smaller number of chisels this meant that a catalogue of carving tools would run to hundreds of varieties and the expert carver had to have most of them (Fig 13C).

Carving tools tended to be lighter than firmer chisels and gouges of the same size. Barrel-shaped handles were general, often turned with different numbers of rings for identification, and with a flat, planed to prevent rolling. It was usual for the width of the tool to taper back slightly from the cutting edge towards the handle. For use the tools were laid with their cutting edges towards the worker, so that he could identify each tool from the shape of its end. A sectioned tray would hold the tools in place and away from each other. Keeping a sharp edge was very important and tools were kept in racks or in a leather or canvas roll, so that edges could not touch. Green baize cloth became popular for tool rolls.

Although for all other purposes chisels and gouges were sharpened inside or outside only, carvers favoured having a slight bevel on the second side. The ability to sharpen perfectly was an essential skill of the carver (Appendix 2).

A tool with an end like two chisels set at an angle to each other to form a V has been used in some crafts. While most woodworkers squared the corners of mortices with an ordinary chisel, the wheelwright favoured a socket-handled tool he called a 'buzz' or 'bruzz', with a right-angled V and sharpened inside (Fig 13D). This was particularly used for the mortices to take spoke ends.

A wood carver had several V tools, made straight or cranked like his other tools, but with the ends at different angles and of different sizes (Fig 13E). A small deep V or gouge section was called a 'veiner', from its use in cutting veins in leaves.

A V tool was also used in timber yards or forests for roughly carving numbers or letters on the ends of felled logs. This was an alternative to a hooked knife (Fig 10C), where there was a preference for cutting on the push instead of the pull stroke. Another alternative, still in use, is the 'scribing iron' or 'tea scribe' (Fig 13F), which was also used for marking casks by the cooper or cellarman. The side piece serves as a hook knife, while the end curved knife can be used either alone for straight lines or with the point as a sort of compass for curves in numbers and letters.

The bootmaker had his own type of gouge, called a 'welt plough' (Fig 13G), cranked and rather lighter than a carving gouge, as it worked on softer material. The clogmaker had his 'pig's foot' (Fig 13H), which was a sort of chisel, with a small notch at the centre, used for removing sole irons when repairing. The notch served as a nail lifter.

The farrier had a 'buffer' (Fig 13J), a sort of double-ended chisel for use with a hammer. The wedge end was used to lift the clenched end of a nail for withdrawal, and the pointed end was used for driving back a nail which could not be pulled back by its head.

Akin to the chisel action is the forming of short round pieces of wood by driving through a round cutter or a hole in a steel plate. Dowels were made this way. A dowel plate was a piece of sheet steel, with holes of several sizes, fixed over a hole in a bench or a stout block of wood (Fig 13K), so that roughly-shaped pieces of wood could be driven through with a mallet. The holes were given a tapered section to provide a cutting edge and clearance as the dowel went through. The rakemaker produced tines from willow and other woods by driving roughly-shaped pieces through a tube cutter, or 'mandrel' mounted on his bench or horse. In its simplest form this was a steel tube, sharpened at the top, but this caused binding and unnecessary friction as the tine goes through. A better tine former was built up, if metal turning facilities were available (Fig 13L). Only the collar was fixed down. Each tine was driven through into a waiting bucket by the following piece of wood.

CHAPTER 6

Saws

The fact that a serrated edge can be used to cut through material may have been found by accident. Examples have been discovered where flint and other stones have been chipped to give a cutting edge made up of a series of teeth. Like many other tools, saws have developed in different parts of the world, with broadly similar end results.

Stone saws have been found in Egypt, Denmark and Switzerland as well as Britain with reasonably regular serrations chipped in their edges. Of course, these would have been more likely to have been used for tearing meat apart than for sawing in anything like the modern manner.

Saws exist which date from the Iron Age and the early civilisations certainly had iron saws. There are references to saws by Isaiah in the Bible. One early Egyptian saw is shaped like a sickle and is fitted into its handle by insertion. It also has a ferrule, showing that the use of a metal band to prevent splitting was an early discovery. This appears to have been used as a saw, although there is a modern Austrian reaping hook of similar shape made with fine serrations to give a sawlike edge, to grip weeds and grass better than a plain knife edge. However, straight bronze and iron saws from early days in Egypt are still in existence, so the principle was understood.

Early Australian tools inset shark's teeth, either by bedding in gum or by lacing, showing some appreciation of the principle of sawing, while not advancing to a high degree of effectiveness, in ripping meat apart. One of the earliest known British saws has an iron blade with crude teeth, set into a horn handle and secured with a thong (Fig 14A).

Early saws must have been used for hacking and tearing their way through material being cut as alternatives to axe or knife. There was no attempt to obtain a regular cut in either direction that would penetrate by making a groove. This appears to have developed slowly and many saws used up to the early Middle Ages must have relied on having teeth of varying shapes and sizes, that were worked through by brute force, and the lucky chance that some of the teeth had correct cutting angles.

No doubt the production of steel of uniform quality and the making of files of reasonable precision helped users to appreciate what made a saw cut. This led to the formation of teeth with the right shapes and of uniform sizes, sharpened to the correct angles. Early saws were without set. Some tapered in thickness so that the cutting edge was thicker than the back and this gave some clearance as the saw worked its way through the wood. Later, the setting of teeth alternately in opposite directions so as to cut a kerf wider than the metal of the saw was discovered. This brought saws, as far as their method of cutting was concerned, to the stage at which they are today.

The inefficiency of saws until only a few centuries ago is seen by the alternative methods of cutting employed rather than depending on a saw. Wood and metal were chopped. Cuts were made part way and the piece broken off. Wood might even be burned away.

With the efficient sharpening of saws had to come a decision on the direction of cut. For some purposes, as when cross-cutting a log, the saw could cut in both directions, but in Britain, and most parts of the world, a saw was, and still is, expected to cut on

Page 85 The top man on a pit saw. The log is held in place by dogs

Page 86 (top) A wooden trying plane at the back, with a wooden jack plane, compared with a modern steel trying plane; *(bottom)* special planes: a fillister with its side gauge towards the camera, an old woman's tooth or router and two moulding planes. In front: a wood-filled metal bull-nose plane, a curved rebate plane and a pair of hollow and round planes

the push stroke. Yet there would be less risk of buckling if the cut came as the blade was pulled. Only the Japanese and Chinese appear to have designed their saws to allow for this, and their saws have teeth arranged to cut this way. Most of these have straight handles and range in size from small hand saws, looking rather like carving knives with teeth (Fig 14B), to quite large rip saws, used by the worker standing on the job. Some of these saws were thicker towards the end, like a butcher's cleaver (Fig 14C).

Some early saws had teeth on both edges, probably due to the desire to make the most of the comparatively valuable metal, or to give alternative cutting edges and lengthen the time between the stops for resharpening. In more recent times saws having teeth on both edges allowed for coarse and fine cuts. As craftsmanship and tool design became more advanced, double-edged saws fell from favour. Today, catalogues may have pruning and plumbers' saws sharpened on both edges, but most craftsmen favour single cutting edges.

Buckling was a problem with early saws, particularly when the metal was bronze, iron or the inferior early steels. One way of preventing this is to tension the saw in a frame. Frame saws for general purposes are still common in many countries today. In the more advanced countries frame saws are only used when a narrow blade is required for cutting curves. The basic frame saw has the blade held by pegs or other means to two bars which act as levers over a central member and are tensioned by drawing the opposite ends of the levers towards each other, usually by twisting a peg through a cord (Fig 14D), by the method nowadays often called a 'Spanish windlass'. Many turns of cord helped to take the load and the tapered peg was locked against the central member. In its simplest form, one of the end pieces was lengthened to make a handle. Handles might be below the blade (Fig 14E), above the cord (Fig 14F) or in both places. The shapes of ends varied from near straight to graceful curves. A

F

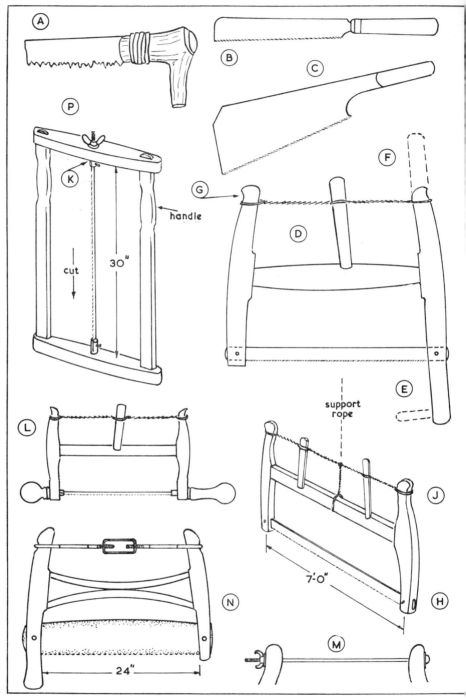

Fig 14 Saws: early and frame types

peg at the handle end might prevent the hand slipping off. A hollowing at the top retained the cord (Fig 14G).

In the simplest form the blade was retained by a steel pin through the wooden end (Fig 14H), possibly with the hole reinforced by metal plates. This was suitable for a fairly wide blade making straight cuts. Stone masons' saws of quite large size were made in this way with the saw hung over the work and lubricated as it cut by water running on the blade. To allow for the great length, two pegs were used to tension the cord (Fig 14J).

In many crafts there was an advantage in having the blade to turn so that curves could be cut. To allow for this in some frame saws the blade was pinned into metal rods, free to turn in holes in the ends of the frame (Fig 14K). In most cases the rods were screwed and nuts could be used to provide tension in addition to that provided by any cord. Modern bow saws use the same idea, but handles are provided on the rods (Fig 14L).

As screwing tackle became available, many frame saws were given metal tensioning arrangements in place of the cord, either by a rod having a wing nut at one end (Fig 14M) or by a turnbuckle at the centre with right- and left-hand threads as seen in the American buck saw, used for cutting up logs (Fig 14N).

Another type of frame saw had the blade centrally, with a screw tensioning arrangement (Fig 14P). This was used while standing with the blade vertical and cutting away from the operator. In the chairmaking trade at High Wycombe this was called a 'Jesus saw', presumably from the constant bowing action when using it.

A metal frame saw was called a 'bettye saw' or 'Dancing Betty' and had a construction very much the same as a modern engineer's hacksaw, but with two widely spaced handles at the top (Fig 15A). This heavy saw with a blade about 18in long was used by cart and carriage makers for cutting curves while the wood was supported on trestles, the handles being on top for a downward cut.

89

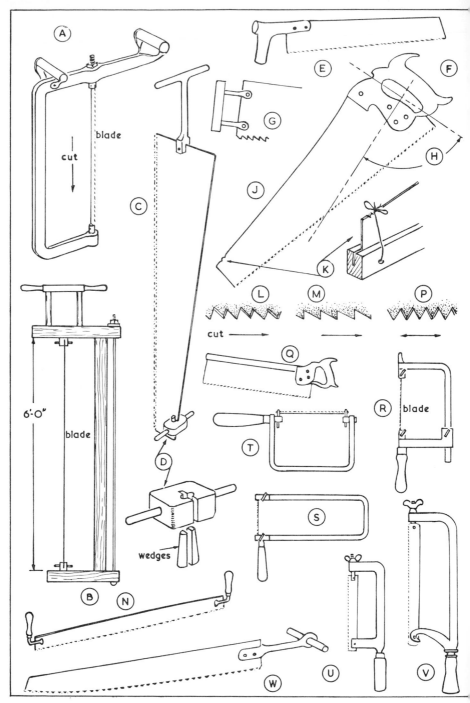

Fig 15 Saws: frame, pit, cross-cut and modern hand types

The wheelwright used an even bigger saw of a generally similar type, made of wood and called a 'felloe saw' (Fig 15B). This was used over a pit, with top and bottom sawyers in the same way as a pit saw, but it could cut curves, in particular the felloes which made up the rim of a wheel. The substantial wooden frame held the tool rigid and tension was by a screwed rod and nut.

Before the days of machinery for converting logs to planks, logs were split for some purposes, but for accurate cutting a 'pit saw' was used. The log was laid over a pit deep enough for a man to stand in, then cut in its length by a pit saw, with one operator standing on the log and his mate in the pit below. For this purpose the saw blade might be anything between 4ft and 10ft long, with very coarse teeth and quite wide, as an aid to maintaining a straight cut (Fig 15C). Various types of top handle were used, but the commonest was a tiller forming a T handle on an extension, so that the top man did not have to bend excessively. As the saw might have to be withdrawn to pass supports or to enter another cut when several passes were made at a time, the bottom handle had to be removable. This was known as a 'saw box' and was held on by wedges (Fig 15D). It had a substantial centre, possibly reinforced by metal, and side handles. Sawyers worked as a team and might be employed by a yard or move from job to job. The bottom man sometimes used perforated zinc to protect his eyes from sawdust. Pit saws are still made in Britain for use in some African countries.

The basic single-handed saw for most woodworking trades in Britain was a piece of steel, tapered and with a hand grip that might be open and hook-shaped in its more primitive form (Fig 15E) or closed (Fig 15F). Simple bar type handles have been found on some saws (Fig 15G), but the shapes common until the simplification with the recent introduction of plastics seem to have been usual for a very long time, with only minor variations. The quirks and twists in their outline contributed nothing except decoration and strength in a few vital places. Beech was the favoured wood for handles. This was fixed with three or more rivets or screws. The best cutting action came from having the grip at right-angles to a line reaching near the middle of the cutting edge (Fig 15H).

The back of the saw might be straight, or Americans favoured the hollow of a 'skew-back' (Fig 15J), which some craftsmen claimed to be superior, but this is difficult to explain. Sometimes a nib was provided near the end of the blade, to retain the string of a sheath made by cutting a slit in a piece of wood (Fig 15K).

Saws of this type were given cross-cut teeth (Fig 15L), sharpened so they cut across the fibres of the wood with something like a knife action in two lines, due to the set of the teeth, if they were intended for general use. For cutting along the grain, the saw was called a 'rip' saw and had teeth which cut with more of a chisel action (Fig 15M), but still with a set so that a wide cut or 'kerf' was made. General-purpose saws tended to be 20in to 26in long, while rip saws might be up to 30in long. For information on sharpening and setting saws see Appendix 2.

Above about 30in long a saw became too large for single-handed use. Even if not too heavy, there was a risk of buckling. Larger saws were made for use by two men, with each man in turn applying power as he pulled. The usual handles stood upright for a two-handed grip, either on permanently-riveted tangs (Fig 15N) or arranged to drop into sockets or bolt directly to the blade. Cross-cut saws were, and still are, made in lengths between 4ft and 7ft. Blades may be wide or narrow. It is easier to maintain a straight cut with a wide blade, but with a narrow blade there is less friction between the blade and the sides of the kerf so effort is less. A variety of teeth are available today, mostly with 'gullets' (spaces) between groups of teeth to clear sawdust, but older saws had peg teeth, $\frac{1}{2}$in or more pitch, sharpened to the same angle each side, to cut both ways (Fig 15P).

There have been cross-cut saws of an in-between size, with a normal handle for single-handed use, but another peg handle which could be fitted on the other end for two-handed use. These saws, of American origin, seem to be more a product of the factory age.

The number of saws in a woodworking craftsman's kit was quite small only a few centuries ago. As the need for more accurate work became evident if something better than rough chests and stools were to be made, finer saws were introduced. The back saw became the more exact woodworker's bench saw. This had a stiffening piece of metal folded along the back and might have had a straight handle, but something like the present day 'tenon saw' soon developed (Fig 15Q). With a blade length of 10in to 16in and 12 to 16 teeth per inch, accurate sawing of joints became possible. A smaller version became known as a 'dovetail saw', but both saws are used for many more jobs than their names imply. The coffinmaker used a similar saw about 24in long to cut a group of kerfs across the inside of the sides of a coffin to allow it to be pulled to a curve. He called it a 'kerfing saw'.

A narrow hand saw could be used for cutting curves. A hand saw which had become narrow through years of sharpening might be kept for this purpose. In more recent times a narrow tapered saw, called a 'pad saw', was produced for curves, made rather thick for stiffness and not so highly tempered so that, if bent, it would not break, but could be pulled back again. An even finer saw, but still soft and thick, was the keyhole saw, used with a straight handle, into which it has been made to retract in modern types. These saws had an advantage over frame saws for internal curves, where the frame saw would have to be dismantled and threaded through a hole.

Very fine saws were beyond the scope of local manufacture, but fine factory-made saws came out of the Midlands during the Industrial Revolution. These were used for piercing, with an adjustable frame that would take short pieces (Fig 15R). This type of saw was used by metalworkers as well as woodworkers. Piercing was also done in horn. The 'fretsaw' developed from this (Fig 15S). It reached its heyday in Victorian days when many suitable and unsuitable things were decorated by piercing. The modern equivalent for shaped work is the coping saw (Fig 15T).

Much cutting of metal was done by chopping while hot, but for accurate fitting, as when building up decorative gates, the metalworker needed a saw. A frame saw, with a replaceable blade, was used at least from the Middle Ages, when screw-cutting became generally possible. An engineer's saw of 1750 (Fig 15U) is not so very different from the hacksaw common today. The blade has little stiffness in itself, but is tensioned by a wing nut. The Lancashire hacksaw, of which there are specimens still in use, is of similar form (Fig 15V). Some metalworking saw blades had their teeth set, but this is difficult with fine teeth. Another way of clearing the kerf was to taper the blade in its thickness towards its back. A type of blade originating in Germany was given a wavy edge so that it cut a kerf wider than the thickness of the metal. Butchers also used frame saws for cutting bones. These were generally similar to engineers' hacksaws.

An ice saw (Fig 15W) was used with the ice axe (Fig 1N) for cutting blocks of ice for preserving food in an ice house. This was something like a small pit saw, but with very large spiked teeth.

CHAPTER 7

Planes

There is no evidence to indicate that primitive man ever devised anything like the tools we now call planes, but they were known to early civilisation, often in a crude form, although remains show that there were planes that would bear comparison with some used today.

Froes, draw knives, and to a lesser extent adzes, are not precision tools. How much wood they remove and how accurately they cut to a desired shape depends on the skill of the operator and the characteristics of the grain of the particular piece of wood. A flaw in the grain or an unnoticed shake in the wood, as well as unsteadiness of hand, could cause an error. For the woodland crafts and for preliminary dividing up of large pieces, this may not matter and in some cases a cut following a curved grain may be desirable. For furniture making, waggon building, wheelwright's work and much general carpentry, a more controlled cut is needed for surfaces to be true and parts to fit.

A plane is a means of putting a restriction on the cut of a blade, usually of the chisel type. Many planes were just this— with a chisel through a hole in a block of wood, wedged or otherwise held so that only a small amount of the cutting edge projected and there was enough clearance for shavings to pass through.

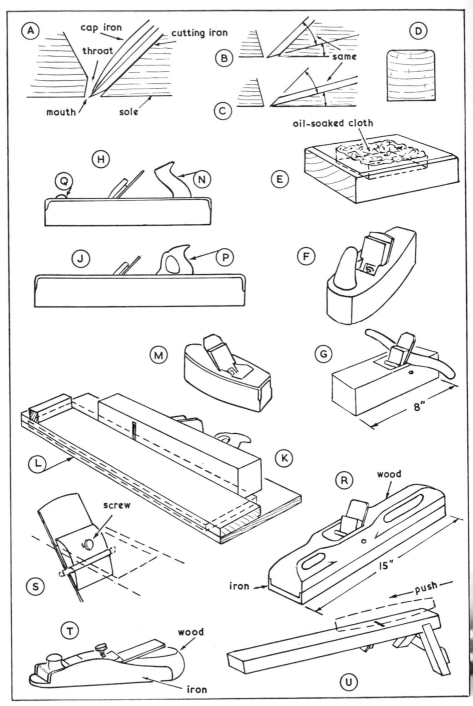

Fig 16 Basic types of planes

Many planes still have single 'irons'. All early planes did. This can tend to tear up the surface, so modern planes only have single irons for work across the grain, cutting grooves and other places where narrow cuts are made. At some undefined point in history, the use of a 'back iron' or 'cap iron' was discovered— probably in the early Middle Ages (Fig 16A). The curved cap iron, set quite close to the cutting edge, has the effect of breaking the shaving as it comes away, so that it cracks across at close intervals. On the surface being worked, this minimises tearing out of the grain, so that fibres are not pulled and the result is a smoother finish.

The cap iron is adjustable, being held to the blade by a screw through a slot. This allows for adjustment as the blade shortens due to sharpening, and the cap iron can be moved closer to the edge for hard woods than it is for soft woods.

The plane 'iron' is still often called that, although the cutting edge must obviously be steel. In modern metal-bodied planes, the thin parallel blade is all-steel, but in wooden-bodied planes, still used and favoured by many craftsmen, the blade may still be iron, with only a thin layer of steel welded on the cutting side (Fig 12B).

The angle of cut is, of course, the V on the end of the blade. In some single-iron planes the blade is mounted with the sharpened bevel side downwards (Fig 16B). In some it is mounted with the bevel upwards (Fig 16C). The effect on the cut on the wood may be the same, unless the blade angle is raised or lowered. Old planes may have their single irons either way, but with a cap iron the bevel has to be downwards. The slot through which the cutting edge projects was known as the 'mouth' and the widened part above it the 'throat'. The bottom was the 'sole'.

Most British general-purpose planes were made of beech, although some special planes might have box or other harder wood at points of wear, as in narrow edges of moulding planes. For filled metal planes, rosewood was often used. Beech remained true in shape particularly if it was cut annularly from the log, so that the grain was horizontal and the medullary rays vertical (Fig 16D). It was hard enough to stand up to the considerable wear imposed on the bottom. Beech was also widely distributed and had little tendency to split or distort. However, a craftsman valued his planes and prepared a new one by soaking it in linseed oil. The mouth was blocked with putty and oil poured in. This was left to soak into the grain and replenished as necessary for a week or more, until oil was seen oozing from the end grain. The effect of this was to prevent the absorption of moisture, which causes warping, and to lubricate the sole. A hollowed block of wood, filled with cotton waste soaked in oil (Fig 16E), would also be kept on the bench and the plane drawn across it occasionally during the day.

Like saws, British planes have nearly always been designed to be pushed, but there are more variations amongst planes than there are amongst saws. Some early sixteenth-century British planes appear to have been arranged so that they could be pulled or pushed. The Germans favoured wooden planes with a horn at the front so that they could be pulled (Fig 16F). These are still in use, but today their craftsmen have to get used to pushing mass-produced steel planes, like the rest of the world. Japanese and Chinese planes were mostly designed to be pulled. Some of their planes had handles at the sides (Fig 16G), rather like spokeshaves, allowing a rather different control with two hands pushing or pulling.

The basic wooden planes, common to many trades, were: the 'jack' plane, about 15in long (with its name from 'Jack of all trades'); the 'trying' (or 'try') plane, about 22in long; the 'shooting'' (or 'shuting'), rather longer; and the 'smoothing' plane, about 8in long. The jack plane (Fig 16H) could be set to take off coarse shavings and bring a surface quickly near to the desired finish. The longer trying plane (Fig 16J) spanned bumps and hollows so it gave a more level and straight surface. The shooting plane was interchangeable with it to a certain extent (Fig 16K), but its particular value came in its use for making long straight edges, as when boards had to be glued edge-to-edge. A shooting board might be used to hold the wood while the plane slid on its side (Fig 16L). The coffin-shaped smoothing plane (Fig 16M) was kept finely set and used for getting the best finish after a surface had been trued by other planes. Cutting edges in these wooden planes were mostly between $1\frac{3}{4}$in and $2\frac{3}{4}$in.

Many early planes were without proper handles, but surviving examples show by their wear how they were held, mostly with the right hand behind the iron and the left hand over the forward part of the plane. More recent smoothing planes were held in this way, if they were intended to be pushed, but some quite small German smoothing planes had a horn for pulling. There are some examples of British smoothing planes with a handle like the larger planes, sunk into the body behind the iron.

Some early handles were simply pegs, but a form shaped to give a comfortable grip was made, either open (Fig 16N) for a jack plane, or closed to give strength (Fig 16P) for the longer planes. Modern factory-produced steel planes have followed closely to the traditional handle design.

Plane irons held by wedges were driven down to make a coarser cut by tapping with a hammer on the top. To retract or remove the iron small planes were hit on the end, or long planes were hit on the top forward of the throat. This momentarily stretched the top of the plane and loosened the wedge and iron. Hitting forward of the throat could be by turning the plane over and tapping it on the bench, but it was more usual to employ a hammer or mallet, and to prevent damage a boxwood button might be let in (Fig 16Q).

Some early craftsmen realised the value of having a metal sole on a plane, as it would not warp and there was some advantage in weight. There are examples of cast bronze and iron bodies filled with wood, dating earlier than might have been expected.

In St Albans Museum there is a jack plane found locally, which was used during the Roman occupation, about AD 60. Its proportions are similar to a modern plane, with a wooden body in a cast iron sole, but with slots to provide hand grips (Fig 16R). The single iron was held by a wedge against a peg through the body and across the throat.

During the eighteenth and nineteenth century cast iron and gunmetal plane bodies, with the bottom machined true, became available commercially for craftsmen to complete themselves and there are some very fine examples still in use, where the country craftsmen have used rosewood and other attractive woods as well as beech to complete their own metal-soled planes. Gunmetal had the advantage of resisting rust, but it was easily dented or scratched.

Some of these planes had driven wedges to hold the irons, but constant hitting was not really suitable for cast iron and many of these soles cracked. A better arrangement used a screw to tighten the wedge (Fig 16S).

A plane small enough to hold in one hand, either entirely cast in metal or with wood filling in metal, had its blade at a low angle and was called a 'block' plane (Fig 16T). The low angle was particularly suitable for cutting across end grain, taking off sharp edges and any light planing.

The cooper used several planes similar in many ways to the bench planes of other craftsmen, but with peculiarities to suit his requirements. Barrel staves were shaped by rubbing on the plane, instead of the plane on the wood. The plane was a long 'jointer', possibly 6ft long and 5in square section, like an inverted trying plane without handles, supported at its forward end by legs (Fig 16U). The operator pushed his wood against the blade.

For levelling the end of a barrel the cooper had a 'topping' or 'sun' plane (Fig 17A). This was like a jack plane with its body made approximately to the curve of the barrel, this giving a

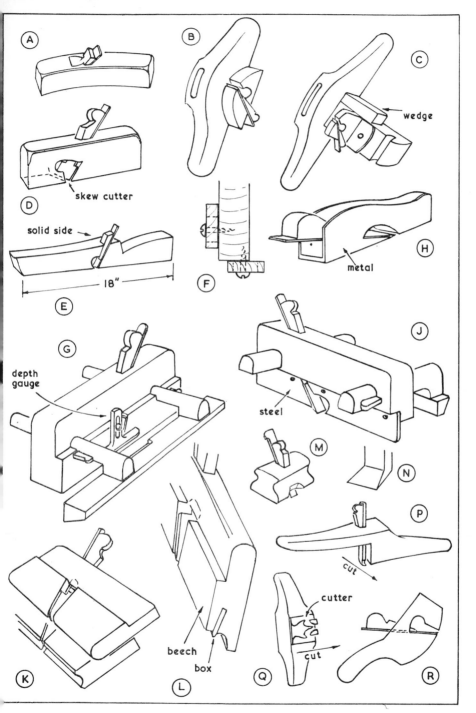

Fig 17 Special planes

greater bearing surface than it would have if the plane had been straight.

To take the barrel heads the cooper had to prepare the insides of the staves with two specialist planes. The 'chiv' or 'chive' (Fig 17B) had a curve to match the particular barrel, so for all sizes produced there had to be a different tool. The purpose of this was to work a broad 'howel' or hollow around the inside of the end of the barrel. The actual cutting part was either like a smoothing plane with a rounded bottom or more of a rebate plane, with the cutter the full width of the stock it was mounted in. The rest of the body acted as a guide and something to hold.

Within this hollow a groove was made to take the edge of the head with a 'croze' (Fig 17C). This might have a narrow plane-type cutter or some of these tools were made with a cutter like a section of saw with several teeth. The final groove was about $\frac{1}{2}$in wide to match the shaped edge of the barrel head. The distance of this groove from the end of the barrel could be adjusted by having the cutter on a sliding piece held by a wedge. Although the curve of a croze was not quite so critical as in the chiv, it was usual to have a separate one for each size of barrel.

With no machinery to work rebates, make grooves or manufacture mouldings, the woodworking craftsman needed a large collection of special planes to do these jobs. Fashions in furniture and architecture called for much moulding and shaping two or three centuries ago and producing all these shapes called for skill in using a multiplicity of planes.

Ordinary planes have their irons about $\frac{1}{4}$in in from each side of the plane, so that the tool could not cut closer than this into an angle or rebate. For planing closer the tool needed its iron right out to one or both edges of the plane. The simple version of this was called a 'rebate' ('rabbet', 'rabbit') plane. The usual construction had a narrow tang behind the blade, held with a wedge and a curved throat to clear shavings (Fig 17D). Widths might be between $\frac{1}{2}$in and $1\frac{1}{2}$in. In some rebate planes the cut-

Page 103 (top) Assorted chair shaves, High Wycombe Museum; *(bottom)* three wood-boring braces: a metal one with bit socket, a wooden one with removable bit holder and a wooden brace with spoon bit

Page 104 (*top*) A shaving horse, with wood in position for shaving with a draw knife; (*bottom*) cleaving brake. Both pictured at the Forestry Commission Mayswood Centre

ting edge was set on the skew. This gave a slightly slicing action to the cut and had the effect of making shavings curl out of the throat, instead of piling up as sometimes happened with a straight blade. One type of Chinese rebate plane had a parallel single iron flush with one side of the plane (Fig 17E) so it could only be used with that side in a rebate. This method of construction also meant that the only strength to prevent the plane body distorting when the wedge was driven was provided by the other side.

Many special planes had their irons arranged like the rebate planes, with the irons bevel-downwards and with notched wedges. In these planes the wedge and iron are slackened by tapping under the notch of the wedge and not by hitting the end of the plane.

A plain rebate plane gives no control over the width or depth of the cut. With a wide sole, a strip of wood may be screwed on temporarily to give control of width and there could be another strip on the side as a depth stop. This was done, but there was obviously a limit to the number of times screws could be driven and a plane developed with stops. This was called a 'side fillister', with the strips controlled by screws in slots, to give adjustment (Fig 17F).

When wood was planed entirely by hand, considerable emphasis was placed on the face side and face edge, from which all measurements were taken. If a rebate had to be cut against one of these faces, the side fillister could be used, but if the rebate was away from the corner between face side and edge, the craftsman preferred a tool that was guided by a face surface. This happened in making windows and cutting rebates for the glass. In this case the width guide is on two crossbars, which are controlled by two wedges. The tool was known as a 'sash fillister', from its use in making sash windows (Fig 17G). Some of these tools had moulded decorated stops and there were brass reinforcements and sliding depth stops. A boxwood

105

sole was sometimes fitted to withstand the concentrated wear on a fairly narrow surface.

A variation on the block plane, with its low-angled iron for work across the grain, had a full width cutting edge. This had an all-metal body or a wood-filled casting and was called a 'shoulder' plane, from its use in trimming the shoulders of wide tenons (Fig 17H). A similar plane, but quite short in front of the cutting edge, was called a 'bull-nose' plane, and was used for getting close into corners of stopped rebates.

A plane generally similar in construction to the sash fillister is the plough (Fig 17J). This has the same sort of side and depth stops, but is designed to cut grooves. A typical plough had a set of eight irons in widths from $\frac{1}{8}$in to $\frac{9}{16}$in. Instead of a sole, the plough had a metal strip of the same width as the narrowest iron. The irons were wedged in the same way as in a fillister or rebate plane and the groove cut was the same as the width of the iron being used. Plough planes of this general pattern have been found dating from the eighteenth century.

There was considerable use made of moulding in decoration and for such things as picture frames, being most prolific in early Victorian England. Without power-driven spindles and other machines to do the work mouldings had to be planed by hand. Fillister and rebate planes removed the bulk of the wood, then special planes made the curved sections. For smaller mouldings one plane might cut the complete shape. Many of these planes were of rebate plane size and general construction. Craftsmen had a set of 'hollows' and 'rounds'. The soles were rounded in cross-section, but straight in their length, and they were named according to the shape they produced. They were kept in matching pairs, in widths from $\frac{1}{4}$in to $1\frac{1}{2}$in (Fig 17K).

When wood was used for making gutters, the plane for working the hollows was of jack plane size and type, but with its bottom rounded in cross-section.

Planes that would cut the complete moulding shape were made of beech, but the better ones had box let in to reinforce where narrow sections were needed (Fig 17L). At one time these were factory-produced in a large range of sizes and patterns. Cutters were held by tangs and wedges in the usual British way. Chinese moulding planes had parallel irons brought close to one edge, as in their rebate planes. For a symmetrical moulding an extra position for iron and wedge was provided, facing the opposite way, to allow for variations in grain.

Modern equivalents of rebate planes, fillisters and ploughs are made in metal, but hollows, rounds and moulding planes are no longer available new.

For levelling the bottom of a groove, particularly across the grain, as when making housing joints for shelves, a plough cutter or chisel was wedged through a block of wood and used with the blade projecting the correct depth. This was called a 'router' or 'old woman's tooth'—even in catalogues (Fig 17M). A wide cutter in a plough plane tended to dig up the bottom of the groove, as it only had a narrow piece of metal in front of it. The router had nothing in front of the cutter, so it would tear up along the grain, but the main use was across the grain and this was satisfactory. Modern routers have a blade which cuts at a flatter angle (Fig 17N).

The coachbuilder used the name 'router' for a different tool. He had the problem of grooving and moulding while following a curve. The tool he used to groove a frame, whether on a straight or curved edge, was his router. The earlier type was called a 'pistol router' from its appearance (Fig 17P). This was a two-handed tool, cutting at right-angles to its length, with a stop below to keep the groove parallel to an edge. This was superseded in 1850 by a French patented side router (Fig 17Q), with a steel central assembly and cutters to work either way at a fixed distance from the edge. For moulding around curves the coachbuilder had tools used in a similar way, but with shaped soles and irons.

For very fine work or special purposes craftsmen made their own small planes, usually called 'thumb' planes. An example is a rebate plane that was made for working on a concave curved edge (Fig 17R). This has a normal rebate plane iron, there is an extension to fit in the palm of the hand and the bottom is reinforced with brass screwed on.

Spokeshaves

A plane may be used in one hand or with one hand ahead of the blade and one hand behind it. If the work is straight in its length, this is the type of tool favoured by Western craftsmen. For some purposes, as when shaping a curve in the length or following an undulating pattern, it is more convenient to have a tool with very little length in its sole and with the handles at each side of the blade. In general, a tool of this type is called a 'spokeshave' today, but country craftsmen had special names for the variations used in their own trades. In some ways a spokeshave is a refinement of the draw knife. Its cutting depth is restricted and this allows greater control to be exercised.

Two types of cut are found in these tools. A low-angled and fairly slim cutter operates almost flat on the wood, with a narrow mouth and throat ahead of it (Fig 18A). The other type is more like a plane, with a high-angled cutter with its bevel downwards (Fig 18B).

From its name, the basic spokeshave was a wheelwright's tool, although it was used for many other jobs besides shaving spokes. Most of these tools had a cutting edge 2in to 4in long and two spurs at the ends were held only by friction in holes (Fig 18C). This is a seemingly crude method of fixing and adjusting, but it works and is still seen in spokeshaves sold today. The same sort of spokeshave was used on leather. Some of these had the tangs threaded and wing nuts gave a degree of

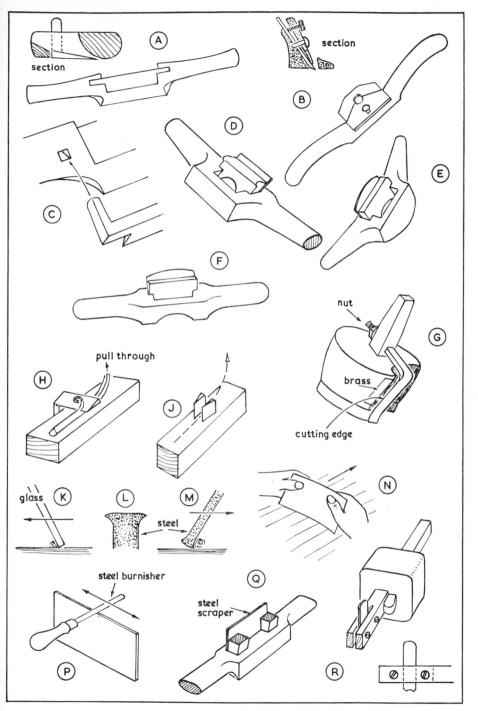

Fig 18 Spokeshaves, special planes and scrapers

adjustment. Small spokeshaves were made of box. Larger ones were lancewood or beech. Not all spokeshaves were the graceful tools produced today. Some old ones, still in existence, are quite satisfactory around the cutters, but elsewhere and at the handles, the shaping and finishing is very crude. The greatest wear was forward of the cutting edge and many well-used shaves had this reinforced with brass.

The chairmaker called his shave a 'travisher'. The one used for finishing work was a 'cleaning off iron'. Chairmakers' shaves with curved cutters and bottoms were used after the adze for finishing the hollow seats and for other chair parts. These shaves were made with the handles raised to clear the worker's knuckles on a broad seat. Normal spokeshaves used on narrow work had their handles almost in line with the cutting edge. Most chair seat shaping was done across the grain, to reduce the risk of tearing out.

The cooper used a tool with a wedged iron and called it a 'downright shave' (Fig 18D). If it had a convex blade for working inside a cask it was called an 'inside shave' (Fig 18E). The wheelwright used a tool of similar construction, with a hollow bottom and blade for rounding spokes. This was called a 'jarvis' (Fig 18F).

A sort of rotary spokeshave was used to clean inside a hole in a cask or other wooden article. This 'round plane' had a body of slightly less diameter than the final hole, with a low-angle cutter having a limited adjustment with a nut and a square iron stock for turning (Fig 18G).

A shave with a type of cutter like a spokeshave was used for removing the inside of split cane 'skeins' for basketmaking and chair seating (Fig 18H). A skein is about a one-third section of round cane which has been cut with a cleaver. The wood base was fixed down and the skein pulled under the cutter to obtain a uniform thickness. Another type of shave had two cutters on edge and the cane was pulled between them (Fig 18J).

Iron spokeshaves have been made for some time. They hold a blade, with bevel downwards, rather like a plane. Some tools have screw adjustments, so they may be considered more scientific, although for fine work many craftsmen still prefer the wooden tool with the low blade. Both types may have flat or curved soles.

Scrapers

A plane or spokeshave cuts and removes a shaving. On some woods the grain is such that a smooth surface cannot be obtained however sharp or carefully-used is the plane or which direction it is used. A scraper may succeed where a plane fails. For a fine finish on a surface which is to be polished, the scraper may follow the plane in any case. This is better than working with any sort of abrasive, as the sanding technique tends to bend over short fibres which will rise again and marr the polish or other treatment.

Scrapers used to be made from broken glass. With the edge tilted and pushed away from the operator, extremely fine shavings were produced when the angle was adjusted correctly (Fig 18K). A steel scraper is merely an oblong piece of steel, similar to that used for saw blades. Pieces of broken saws were used in the past. The cutting edge is filed square and further rubbed down with an oilstone. This burrs the edge (Fig 18L) and it is this turned-out burr which is used as a cutting edge when scraping (Fig 18M). On a flat surface, the scraper is held by the ends with the thumbs forcing it into a slight curve as it is worked forward at an angle (Fig 18N). Scraping may be in any direction on the surface.

The edge may not last long before the tool fails to cut, caused by the burr turning back. The edge may be restored by rubbing with a hard round steel burnisher (Fig 18P) or the flat of a chisel. Eventually, a new edge has to be made with file and oilstone.

For general wood finishing as in furniture making, the scraper was held in the hand. Tools have been devised in which the scraper was mounted in spokeshave-type handles, which held it at the correct angle and forced the slight curve needed. The chairmaker called such a tool, a 'devil'. The cooper called his a 'buzz' (Fig 18Q). These were of wooden construction, but there is a modern steel type in which the curve of the scraper can be adjusted by a screw.

Shallow moulding or hollowing can be done by scraping. A common arrangement was a tool like a marking gauge, with a split end to take a scraper blade (Fig 18R) sometimes called a 'scratch stock'. Two screws held the blade. The scraper could be shaped to scratch a beaded design. A plain end could scratch a groove to take a length of veneer banding. The same idea has been found in much larger and cruder tools, used to provide shallow decoration on furniture and waggons.

CHAPTER 8

Making Holes

Primitive man probably made the first holes by pushing a sharp stone or piece of wood through an animal skin. Neolithic bone perforators or spikes have been found. Craftsmen today, working in leather, fabric and other soft materials, still do basically the same thing with a spike. Most craftsmen in harder materials also have a use for a spike of some sort. Even the blacksmith punching holes in hot metal is using the same principle.

Pressing a spike or hitting a punch into anything produces a hole by pushing material aside, either by distorting it or stretching fibres. Sometimes this is an advantage, but more often it is necessary to remove some material to achieve a hole of sufficient size. In early days the only way to make a larger hole would have been to tear it away with a sharp stone or bone if it was soft material, or hack it out with a stone axe if it was wood. Another way of dealing with wood was to burn it away. Using a red hot steel rod is not unknown today as a means of piercing wood.

A knowledge of the cutting edges needed for drilling wood and metal seems to have lagged behind that shown in the development of other techniques for dealing with these materials. While craftsmen could produce accurate shapes

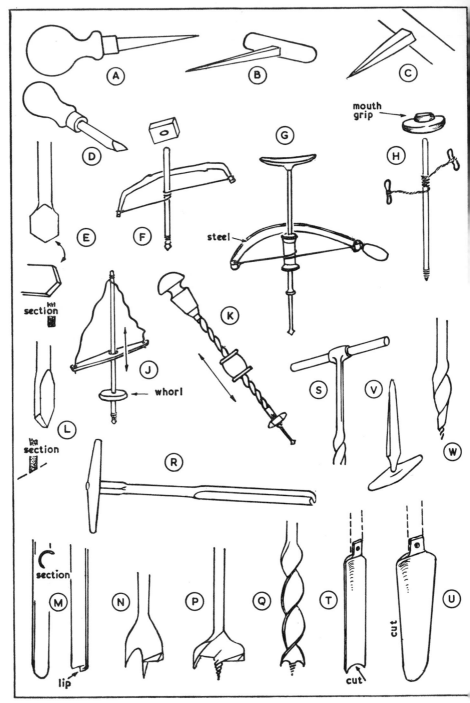

Fig 19 Early means of drilling and drill bit forms

externally and obtain good surfaces with tools of reasonable design, those tools used for making holes had unscientific cutters and the resultant holes were often ragged and untrue. Brute force played a large part in getting through, with the cutter only 'worrying' its way into the material, often with a tendency to split it also. A ragged hole might provide a grip on a nail or dowel, but for a clean finish the hole would have to be finished with other tools.

A plain pointed tool (Fig 19A) was pushed through with a handle or used as a punch with a hammer. The basketmaker's 'bodkin' is an example of a long pointed and handled awl. Giving the awl a tapered squared section scraped away a little more. A tool of this form, with a cross handle (Fig 19B), was called a 'reamer' or 'rimer' and used to open out or taper small holes. Something of more dagger action (Fig 19C) could be used to whittle a way through wood to make a hole of uneven shape. No doubt some daggers were used for this more peaceful purpose. There are records of flint, bone and shell being lashed to the end of a spindle, for use in drilling. A length of leather or skin, used wet and allowed to dry and shrink, would make a sufficiently secure attachment.

Giving the end of a steel spike or bit a chisel shape (Fig 19D) was a move towards a proper cutting edge to break wood fibres as it rotated. This is still found in the woodworker's bradawl.

Early bits were given an end very much like the modern metalworking countersink bit (Fig 19E), both for working wood and metal. As many early means of turning the bit caused it to revolve alternately in opposite directions, the cutting edges were sharpened square across the end, so that they cut equally well (or badly) in both directions. This sort of 'diamond-pointed' bit has the advantage of making a hole larger than the shaft, so friction around the sides of the hole as it deepens is avoided. Against that, there is no guidance from the sides of the bit, and a hole might wander as it gets deeper.

In a fibrous material, like wood, this sort of bit does not sever fibres around its circumference, so the hole becomes very rough and there is a tendency to produce a bursting action, which could lead to splitting.

Primitive man produced fire by friction, using a stick rotated between his hands or by working it with a bow. This type of drive was adapted for drilling. There are pictures of drills worked this way dating from the Egyptian civilisation, at least 800 BC (Fig 19F). The same idea has been used by North American Indians, South Sea Islanders and Eskimos in more recent times. A more sophisticated bow or 'fiddle' drill is in Cheltenham Museum, with a shaped top to lean against and a handled metal bow working a cord around a sort of cottonreel (Fig 19G). An alternative to the use of a bow was to support the stick with a mouth piece and pull the thong backwards and forwards with the hands (Fig 19H). There are examples of bow drills showing signs of having had stones or shells lashed on as bits.

While bow drills and lathes may still be found in India and elsewhere, they never survived in Britain, but another type dating from early days still has its uses. This is the 'pump drill', worked by moving the crossbar up and down so that the spindle rotates alternately in each direction as the thong winds and unwinds. The 'whorl' acts as a flywheel (Fig 19J). Early examples had shell or stone cutters and wood or stone whorls. A modern version, exactly the same in principle, has a metal whorl or weights on the end of a crossbar, and a chuck to hold a bit. It is used in jewellery work and for china repairing. Of course, this can only be used for small holes, but within its scope it provides more power than many other ways of boring small holes, so pump drills were used by many craftsmen. Very early stone whorls have been found, which were used on sticks for spinning wool. These may have provided the idea for giving impetus to drills. Pump drills have been adapted to give a one-way rotation, by having a clutch, so that the flywheel keeps the drill rotating on the return stroke of the handle.

Another alternately-rotating drill was the Archimedian drill beloved of fretworkers towards the end of the Victorian era (Fig 19K). The chuck was a split, screwed end able to hold a small drill with a square stock. With pressure on the top by one hand, the slider was moved up and down the steep threaded part to cause the drill to rotate. Like the pump drill, better tools might have a clutch and balls on a crossbar to serve as a flywheel, giving one-way rotation. However, most of these drills were used with small diamond-pointed bits to make holes for the insertion of piercing saw blades in enclosed work.

As the advantages of a drill bit cutting one way only became appreciated, it is interesting to note that a clockwise rotation, viewed from above, became accepted as the preferred way, all over the world. If the top of the tool is held in the left hand and turning done with the right, this may be logical in some cases, but there is no reason why a drill bit should not be designed to turn continuously the other way. With continuous turning, the diamond-pointed bit could be given more of a cutting edge (Fig 19L). This made it cut faster and more efficiently, particularly in metal, but there was still nothing to clean the circumference of the hole when drilling wood.

It is uncertain when the common woodworker's centre bit came into use. It was preceded however by the 'shell' or 'spoon' bit. For many woodworking crafts, the spoon bit was the standard type (Fig 19M), shaped like a gouge, with the outer curve following the circumference of the hole. This had the advantage of severing the fibres as it progressed and making a clean hole. As the bit was the same size several inches back from the cutting edge, it kept the hole straight for a useful depth. The spoon bit cut the circumference of the hole and most had a lip to scoop out the waste wood. The diamond-pointed drill cut only the body of the hole. At some time—at least by the eighteenth century—someone realised that two actions were needed in drilling wood: a cut around the circumference and a means of scooping away the waste wood. The centre bit does this with a long spur at the centre to guide it, a spur to cut the circumference and a nib knife to lift waste (Fig 19N). This has been the basic carpenter's bit ever since, although chairmakers and others continued to favour the spoon bit.

Spoon bits and centre bits can be forged by hand. Diameters ranged from $\frac{1}{4}$in to about 2in. As factory production of tools came into being, improved bits became available. A centre bit with a fluted gullet to clear waste and a screw centre to pull the bit into the wood and relieve the worker of some of the need to apply pressure, gave quicker and cleaner cutting (Fig 19P).

One snag with a centre bit is its tendency to follow the grain instead of going straight into the wood, as there is no guide behind the cutting part. An early type designed to provide guidance as the drill penetrated was known as the 'Jennings pattern', with two spurs and a twisted flat section (Fig 19Q). Several variations of this idea were, and still are, produced. The 'Irwin pattern' of American origin, has a solid centre and a greater clearance for the waste wood chips.

For most of the development of boring tools throughout the centuries, the drill bit and the means of turning it have either been one piece or the two parts have been permanently joined together. There have been bits which fitted into sockets or some other means of allowing removal, but for woodworking, particularly with spoon bits, each size bit often had its own brace, so a craftsman might possess a rack of braces with different sizes of bits.

In general, the name 'auger' is given to a boring tool with a cross handle at the top and the name 'brace' to a tool with a sweep handle, but there are exceptions. A 'shell auger' is a spoon bit with an extension to a crossed handle (Fig 19R). This might have been square into a wooden handle, or a better and more recent type had a socket with the handle through it (Fig 19S). The Jennings pattern bit was also used to make augers.

Tree trunks were hollowed to form pipes, using another variation on the shell auger. A hole of considerable length could be made by working from opposite ends, with the shell auger being on the end of a long iron rod with a lever top, so that two men could make and enlarge a hole along the grain. A parallel-sided spoon auger, sharpened on the end, was first put through to make a hole about 2in diameter (Fig 19T). This was followed by several shell augers in increasing sizes. These tapered and were sharpened on the side—the small end fitting the hole made by the previous one and the large end opening it out by perhaps an inch (Fig 19U). A series of four augers could produce a hole about 6in diameter through something like 10ft of tree trunk.

Where a short tapered hole was needed, as for the ends of ladder rungs or rake tines, the tapered shell auger might fit a brace or have its own handle (Fig 19V). Although this might make its own hole, it was less labour to use it to follow a pilot hole made by another drill. The cooper used an auger cutting on its side to clean bung holes and called it a 'thief'.

Another bit which has persisted despite its inefficiency is the gimlet, either as a bit to fit a brace or, more often, as a tool with a cross handle (Fig 19W). As the screw centre pulls into the wood a body of increasing width, there is a bursting and splitting action. Although the smallest sizes might have had some use in making holes for nails or screws, they are still listed in sizes up to $\frac{3}{8}$in, when the risk of splitting must be very great.

The wheelwright had to make quite a large hole through the centre of the massive elm hub of a wheel to take the cast iron box which turned on the axle. At one time a hole was made with an auger, then enlarged with chisels and gouges, but a tool was developed, called a 'boxing engine' (Fig 20A), to bore out a true circle. The screwed part was passed through the auger hole and the three-pronged grip engaged. Its teeth held the device cen-

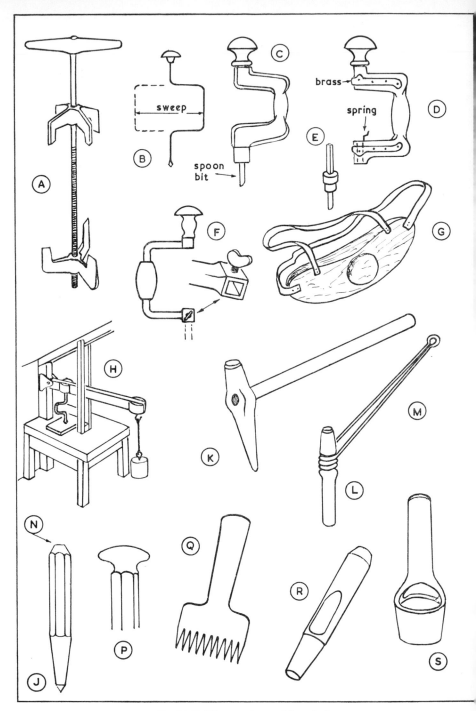

Fig 20 Drilling and punching devices

trally on the underside. When the handle was turned the screwed rod pulled the cutter through the wood to make the hole.

Braces

The brace, still commonly used in wordworking, does not appear to have such a long history as the other methods of drilling, but it was certainly used in the Middle Ages and there are braces still in existence dating from the sixteenth century. Wooden braces with spoon bits were little changed until the late nineteenth century, and old specimens may still be found in country workshops.

Basically, a brace has a means of holding a bit, or the bit is permanently fixed to it or is part of it. In line with this is a knob handle, free to revolve, and power is provided by a sweep handle (Fig 20B). For holes of large diameter there is an advantage in a long sweep so as to give maximum power (up to 14in). Smaller bits can be turned quicker with a short sweep (down to 4in). Where braces were permanently linked to a particular bit, this was allowed for, except that in braces made from solid wood there was the problem of weak short grain in the arms, so these had to be kept as short as possible.

Woodworking braces were normally cut from solid wood (Fig 20C), usually one of the close-grained and heavy hardwoods grown in Britain, such as hornbeam and box, although there are examples of ebony braces, showing that imported woods found their way into workshops. By making the arms thick, sufficient strength could be found in the short cross-grain, but this gave a rather clumsy appearance to the brace. Even then, metal reinforcement might be used (Fig 20D). Some attractive old braces are finished very beautifully with brass reinforcements.

Fixing a bit into the brace seems to have been the weak link. A spoon bit was mostly fixed by wedging. It did not usually have anything like the tapered square end of modern bits. A

H

specimen seen at High Wycombe had a bit mounted in a wooden stock with a square end to fit into the brace, so that bits in their stocks could be changed (Fig 20E). A spring clip retained the square piece. The knob end of a brace was turned and able to rotate on a peg although there are some of these braces with fixed knobs which must have been uncomfortable to hold. For the hand on the sweep the wood was rounded. None of these braces had a loose handle in this place, as found on modern braces.

As might be expected, a blacksmith made his brace of iron or steel. Some of these braces found their way into woodworking trades when the bit was given a square tapered shank, fitting into a socket, where it might have been held by a screw with a wing head (Fig 20F). A waggon builder had to turn large and long bits into hard wood. For this he favoured the smith's type of square socket brace, even after the modern chuck type of brace became available.

Woodworking braces were often crude, with the bit rotating out of line with the handle, and pressure had to be applied continuously to keep it cutting. This meant leaning on the brace and, to spread the load, craftsmen wore a wooden breast bib (Fig 20G) with straps over the shoulders. Chairmaking required a lot of boring of holes and the breast bib was worn as something of a status symbol by the more skilled craftsmen.

A metalworker could not hope to drill anything larger than perhaps $\frac{1}{8}$in in iron or steel with hand pressure. For larger holes a blacksmith had a beam drill (Fig 20H). This was a brace with a large sweep and a square socket for a diamond-pointed drill. The upper end was held under a beam, kept in place by a guide and with weights at the end. The brace was turned by hand. The weights gave enough pressure to keep the drill cutting, or they could be assisted by hand pressure on the beam. For at least a century, up to the early nineteenth century, this laborious method was the only way of drilling large holes in metal.

A drill working through iron can become so hot as to have its temper drawn, even at slow hand speeds. Nowadays, special soluble oils are used to keep the drill cool, but for hand work a boy stood by to dab on oil with a brush; the favoured oil being linseed.

The beam drill was followed by the factory-produced hand drilling machine, with a chuck to hold the drill, and a pawl-and-ratchet type of automatic feed to keep the drill cutting. Precision-made American Morse-pattern drills made other methods of metal drilling obsolete at the end of the nineteenth century.

Holes in stone were avoided as much as possible, because of the difficulty of making them, for some stones would wear the tool away as rapidly as the stone was cut. In softer stone a brace and bit with a diamond shape could be used. For harder stones a hole might be chopped out rather than bored. For hard stones and for glass, holes could be made with a tube having its end fed with an abrasive and oil or water—a modern version of primitive man's piece of cane fed with water and sand, which he rotated to form the handle socket in a stone axe head. A hard abrasive grit, used on the end of a metal tube, can penetrate very hard substances.

For making holes in stone, another tool was a piece of steel tube, given a serrated sawlike end, which was hammered and turned by hand to dig its way into the stone. The modern development of this is the power percussion drill, with a special alloy tip.

Punches

Punches were used for making or starting holes. A deep dent with a punch before starting a drill in metal guided the bit into the right place and cleared the centre of the hole. For a diameter equal to the thickness of the metal in a diamond-pointed bit, or even the centre of a modern Morse-pattern twist bit, there is no actual cut. The dot from a punch took care of this while the drill started cutting. A steel 'centre punch', with its end about 60° (Fig 20J), would have been used for starting a drill in metal, from quite early times. A spike might be used for a similar purpose when starting a bit in wood.

The smith used a punch on hot metal over a hole in his anvil. This punch was tapered, if it were intended to force the hole open by spreading the metal apart (Fig 20K). It was nearer parallel and square across the end if it were intended to push out a portion of metal (Fig 20L). Both types of punch might have a wooden handle, fixed in the same way as a hammer handle. There might be an iron handle, made from light rod wrapped around (Fig 20M), or a similar handle might be made with hazel rod. The hazel rod had the effect of reducing shock on the holder's hand.

Tools frequently hit by a hammer tend to burr over at the top. This was reduced or delayed by grinding a taper on the top of the tool (Fig 20N). A mason used many punches and chisels generally similar to those of the smith and other workers, but he preferred to use a mallet. As this was softer than the tool being hit, the tool head was broadened to spread the area of contact and reduce damage to the mallet (Fig 20P).

A rotating tool will not perform on leather. Saddlers and other leatherworkers use punches to make holes. Awls of various sizes will make holes for sewing, but pricker punches with many points ensure even spacing (Fig 20Q). A craftsman had these punches in several varieties of spacing. Larger holes could be punched out with a sharpened tube. For holes such as are needed in a belt, a series of hollow punches were used. The circle of leather removed was forced up through the centre and ejected through a slot in the side (Fig 20R). Recognised sizes of factory-made punches were, and still are, identified by numbers. No 6 makes a $\frac{3}{16}$in hole and 1 to 5 are less than that. Sizes then go up in $\frac{1}{32}$in steps to No 22, which makes a 1in hole. There are similar punches for making oval holes, as needed for fitting buckles. Larger oval punches, known as crew punches, are for long oval holes in harness parts.

A punch of a different construction is known as a wad punch (Fig 20S). Its smaller sizes overlap on the sizes of ordinary punches, but it is better for larger holes in leather and is now made in sizes up to 3in diameter.

Tinsmiths and workers in pewter used punches very similar to those used for leatherwork, but with more obtuse angles to suit the harder materials.

A hollow punch has to be used over something with enough support to allow the punch to penetrate the leather or metal, yet not so hard as to blunt the cutting edge as it passes through. The end grain of wood had possibilities and a pad was made up from hard wood pieces, or the end of a log was used. Lead was used, particularly for punching tinplate or pewter. A bolster could also be made with hardwood faced with copper or brass. Plier-type hollow punches are fairly modern. With the squeeze action of the punch against a brass pad, they have the advantage of one-hand operation in any position, without having to take the work to a bench.

CHAPTER 9

Holding and Handling

The basic supporting device is, of course, the hand, and primitive man must have held the job in one hand while chopping or otherwise working it with the other hand, possibly supplementing the hand hold by resting the job on the ground or against a tree trunk. A tree trunk has many advantages—in particular its capacity to absorb shocks so that there is little rebound from blows. A section of tree trunk is still the favoured working surface for many crafts. Woodland craftsmen chop on it. Makers of beaten metalwork shape bowls in hollows carved in the end grain. The blacksmith has his anvil spiked to a tree trunk. Leatherworking, and other, punches may be used on the end grain of a tree trunk. End grain of hard wood stands up to considerable use as shown in the butcher's chopping block.

The farrier uses an iron tripod to support the horse's hoof (Fig 21A). The blacksmith also made iron stands for various equipment. One example was a sort of table on which decorative work could be shaped, with the top sufficiently substantial to allow for drilling to take pegs and brackets which hold the parts of a gate, or other wrought ironwork, in shape.

A rather similar idea in wood was used for the shaping of Windsor chair backs. The substantial base was drilled, something like a modern peg board, and the bow for the chair back

126

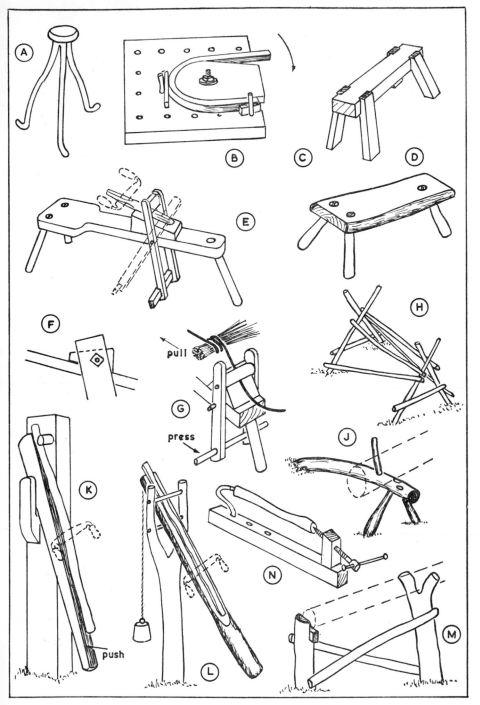

Fig 21 Supports and holding devices

was pulled around a jig and held by wedges against pegs (Fig 21B).

Many craftsmen did much of their work on a trestle at a height that could be used for sitting on, or for sawing or chopping. The general name for this was a 'horse'. It could have four splayed legs, notched into the sides of a top (Fig 21C). While this was a good tool for a precision woodworker on a flat floor, the woodland craftsmen favoured three legs, fitted into holes (Fig 21D). Four legs will wobble on an uneven surface, but three will stand firm anywhere.

Many craftsmen had permanent attachments to the horse to suit their needs, such as a ring for the clogmaker's knife or a fitting for the tool for making rake tines. The edge of the horse was notched by the farrier, who sat astride to file nail points. A development, common to many crafts, was the shaving horse, found in grades between extreme crudity to almost cabinetmaking quality. The basic idea was for the worker to sit astride and press forward with his feet to grip the job (Fig 21E) which was shaved towards him. The most common need was for a grip on something which had to be frequently moved around as it was shaved or otherwise worked. For such a purpose this was quicker than any modern screw-acting vice.

Most shaving horses still in existence show that all sizes were made and the wood was often massive. Some show a lack of appreciation of the principle of levers. The further the footrest is from the pivot compared with the distance from the pivot to the gripping surface, the better will be the grip for a given foot pressure. Most shaving horses had this advantage, but some had very little leverage on the foot side of the pivot.

A shaving horse used by the chair bodger for preliminary shaping chair legs and rungs with a draw knife had a wedge-shaped piece to work on. The seat had two legs under it and the third was some distance away (to give a firm base) at the other end. As the work was never very wide, the horse was narrowed to a near-parallel shape. In most cases the rocking part pivotted on a rod or bolt through the horse top. The crossbar at the top might also be bolted or tenonned on. Using a bolt allowed the bar to swing and present a flat face to the work being held (Fig 21F). The chair bodger was shaping green wood, likely to be slippery with sap. For extra grip he inserted steel teeth into the cramping block. Other craftsmen using a shaving horse included the trug basketmaker, who held ash or chestnut split rods for the basket frame to true their inner surfaces with a draw knife or spokeshave. The thin pieces of willow to form the basket might also be held for shaving in the same way. Willow strips for coracle ribs were held for shaving in a horse. The broom squire pointed handles to push into bundles of birch twigs in a shaving horse and used the shaving horse idea to grip split cane, willow or, later, wire, when binding bundles of twigs (Fig 21G).

Sawing trestles, as used today (Fig 21H), were not so common in Britain, although they seem to have been standard in pioneer America. Instead, the British woodland craftsman favoured a pair of three-legged 'dogs', with the main parts fairly stout curved logs. The wood being sawn rested against a peg (Fig 21J) on each dog. If set up semi-permanently, the end of each main leg was buried in the ground.

The word 'brake' or 'break' was used as the name of a support, but it was not the same thing to all craftsmen. Those who had to work on long strips used a post as a brake. The maker of hoops for dry casks split and pared hazel poles in this way. Long handles needed this support for paring. One type was on the side of a post (Fig 21K). By pressing the bottom of the job or the sloping support piece with the knee or foot, the strip being worked was tightened against a peg. Another form used the same idea, but with two wooden pegs across the top of a forked pole. A weight hanging at the back helped to release the job when foot pressure was released (Fig 21L). A shaving brake for

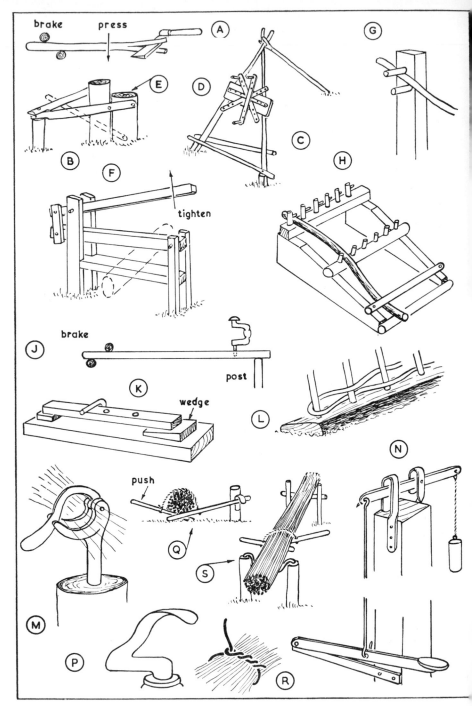

Fig 22 Holding, forming and compressing equipment

stouter pieces, which were more conveniently shaved nearer horizontal, used two posts (Fig 21M). For more precise work on such jobs as axe handles, the wood was supported between two centres, similar to a lathe, except that the screwed end was angled downwards to keep it out of the way of the draw knife or other tool (Fig 21N).

A 'cleaving brake' was used to hold wood being split with a froe. The actual structural arrangements depended on what was to hand in the coppice, but basically a cleaving brake had two arms at an angle to each other, and the lower one nearer the operator. The wood being worked was put between the arms and downward pressure at the working end held it there (Fig 22A). Uprights might be driven into the ground (Fig 22B) or a tripod structure built (Fig 22C). The hoopmaker also had an arrangement of movable pegs in crossbars on the tripod/easel, around which he was able to bend circles of different sizes (Fig 22D). A post, on which to start cleaving, might be built in (Fig 22E). A more elaborate cleaving brake, but probably no more efficient one, looked like a stile (Fig 22F). Pressure was put on by pushing up the top arm. A piece of wood jammed under its end held it there. This had more of a vice effect, so there was no need to keep a downward pressure on the wood that was being worked.

The two-crossbar type of brake was used for straightening or bending poles, although a 'setting brake', consisting of stout pegs in a post, was wide enough for this purpose (Fig 22G). Natural poles which had to be straightened could be levered between these pegs, while those which had to be bent could be given preliminary twists. Where considerable curve had to be given, as in the ash sneads for scythes, the wood was steamed and a number were bent together in a frame (Fig 22H). In making gate hurdles several holes have to be bored. The hurdlemaker uses his cleaving brake and a post to support the wood being bored (Fig 22J). Another device for holding a strip of wood being bored or morticed has an iron hook, so that a supporting block and a wedge force the wood upwards (Fig 22K).

Some craftsmen needed a holding device which was also a pattern or template. A wattle hurdlemaker had a length of log as a mould, set in the ground, with holes at the right spacing to hold posts ('sails') during assembly of the hurdle (Fig 22L). A trug basketmaker built up his basket on a framing table, with posts to hold the elliptical shape. A hoop maker used pegs on his easel (Fig 22D), or he had blocks on a board or horse.

A type of brake to take wood vertically was generally similar to the basic brake, but when made to hold wood being cleft with a froe and beetle it was called a 'monkey'.

Most outdoor craftsmen were workers in wood and it is natural that their holding devices should be made in the material they were used to, but the blacksmith was called in for some things. Screws would seem, today, to provide the best means of applying pressure, but the accurate means of making matching screw threads is only about one century old, and holding devices had to be devised which avoided them. For the besom broom maker, the smith made a type of vice with a swinging hand or foot action to compress the bundle of twigs together (Fig 22M). Another type of post vice used the foot for pressure and a hanging weight for release (Fig 22N). For the clogmaker the smith made a 'steady' (Fig 22P), not very different from the 'foot' used today by shoe repairers.

Levers were used in the woodman's 'deadman's grip' (Fig 22Q) for pulling together bundles of hazel or willow rods. The two rods, joined by a rope or chain, were crossed under the bundle. With one end hooked under the metal strap on a post, pressure with foot or hand on the other end, pulled the bundle together while it was tied. Before the days of cord in plentiful supply, a willow band was twisted up in what is now called a 'timber hitch' (Fig 22R). Another application of this principle was used for chestnut spiles, with the advantage of having the

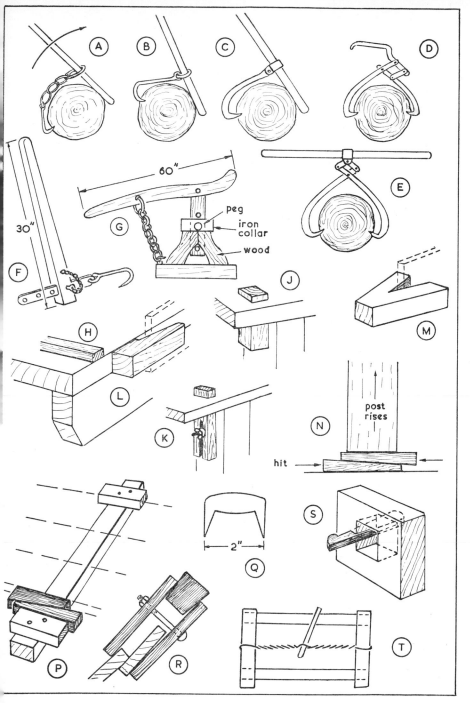

Fig 23 Heavy handling gear and cramping devices

bundle off the ground, resting on two crossbars or metal loops—old bucket handles (Fig 22S). Kneeling on the ends of the poles tightened the bundle and left the hands free for tying.

Weights too great for lifting directly were shifted by levers. Similar equipment is used by woodmen today. A hooked spike on a chain can be used to roll a log (Fig 23A). If a spike is long enough the 'log dog' can be used without the chain (Fig 23B). A more advanced manufactured cant hook is fixed to the pole and the spike pivots (Fig 23C). 'Lazy tongs' provide a grip for lifting logs, either with a single handle (Fig 23D) or with a pole for several lifters (Fig 23E). The wheelwright's 'spoke dog' (Fig 23F) had a family likeness to the log dog, but was adjustable. It was used for pulling spokes into place when fitting the felloes.

The wheelwright needed a jack to lift a waggon when changing a wheel or making a repair. One version has a long lever supported on a post adjustable in height by a peg through holes, with everything massive and a chain provided to hold the lever when the load was raised (Fig 23G).

Most of the equipment so far described was used outdoors. Craftsmen working indoors favoured a bench at table height. This tended to be massive in construction, which must have given a very solid feel with good deadening of rebound when hitting work. A lower well to retain tools behind the main working surface was usual for woodworkers.

Wood was planed against a stop which might be just a strip on the bench top (Fig 23H). A better idea was a square piece through the bench and against a leg (Fig 23J), usually held by friction and hit up or down, but a screw through a slot was a refinement (Fig 23K).

With the inability to make mating threads for screwed parts or a reluctance to use the inaccurate ones produced, much use was made of a wedge action for tightening and applying pressure. A piece of wood can be held against the side of a bench with a block of wood with a tapered notch (Fig 23L), or it can

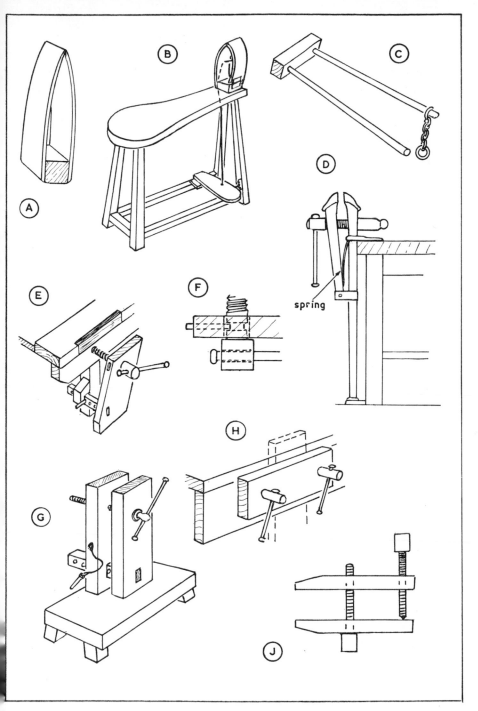

Fig 24 Vices and cramps

be held on edge on top of the bench by V-shaped block (Fig 23M). A pair of 'folding wedges' (Fig 23N) can exert considerable pressure when driven against each other. Put under a post, they will lift it under a load, or they can press boards being glued together (Fig 23P). Driving a single wedge against a peg (Fig 21B) serves to bend things, but folding wedges have the advantage of keeping the pressure parallel.

A joiner's dog was a smith-made device for pulling boards together, due to the wedge shape of the inner faces (Fig 23Q). A longer and larger dog, but working in the same way, was used to secure a log when it was pit sawn. If the two points were in planes at right-angles to each other it was a 'sawyer's hitch' instead of a 'sawyer's dog'.

Wedges were used to exert pressure some way from an edge by a device used by boatbuilders, even today, but also used by other craftsmen (Fig 23R). The two boards are loosely bolted or otherwise joined. When the wedge is driven, pressure is put on the other end. If the wedge end is the longer, there will obviously be a gain in leverage.

Simple wedges are found in the method of fixing plane irons, sliding gauges and other tools, where screwed fittings are used today. A wedge with a knobbed end to retain it can be put in a slot before the sliding part is inserted, so it cannot come out (Fig 23S).

Cord or rope may be tied around a job and tightened by driving wedges under the turns, but the method of tightening by twisting with a stick was used for cramping. Its modern name is 'Spanish windlass'. The idea is seen in the bow saw family (Fig 14). For pulling parts together, several turns are put on, then a stick or hammer handle is used to twist, preferably arranged so that it can be lodged against something when sufficient pressure has been applied (Fig 23T).

The saddler used a clamp, made of two springy thin pieces of wood, fixed to a block and held between his knees (Fig 24A), to

136

Page 137 (*top*) A log dog and chain for rolling a log with a pole; (*bottom*) tongs or hooks for lifting and carrying logs

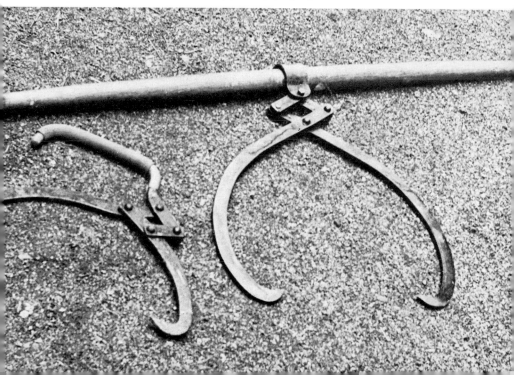

Page 138 (top) A wooden screw for a bench vice, compared with a steel screw for the same purpo
(bottom) marking out tools: trammels at the back, then a try square, a modern mortice gauge, a c
ting gauge, a marking gauge and a wedged mortice gauge. In front: outside and inside calipers, a centre-squa
a scratch stock or scraper gauge, a carpenter's marking knife and dividers or compasses.

keep pieces of leather together while being sewn. Glovers and other leatherworkers used similar clamps, but there were also more refined versions in the form of vices, having the jaws operated by a foot pedal. In one type, there was a padded seat and the foot pedal closed the vice via a thong, then it could be locked down against a serrated metal piece (Fig 24B).

The thatcher needed some means of drawing a load of straw together so that it could be carried up a ladder without loss. One form of carrier was a large forked stick, with the straw put in the fork and the ends pulled together with a cord. A made-up version had two natural round rods let into holes in a block, then the ends pulled together with a chain, after loading with straw (Fig 24C).

The blacksmith favoured a vice made from wrought iron which was able to stand up to hammering without the risk of cracking inherent in most cast vices. The basic form has not changed much over about two centuries. A leg transfers some of the load to the floor and helps in withstanding levering actions. A coarse-threaded screw draws in the hinged front arm, which now has a spring to open it. In the better vices, the projecting screw is protected by a hood at the back of the vice (Fig 24D). As a locally-made product, this type of vice was also used by other craftsmen—the woodworkers making wooden covers for the jaws.

Of course, a screw action vice (American 'vise') is very convenient for a cabinetmaker, joiner or other precision woodworker. The modern worker has at least one and may wonder how his ancestors managed without. The adapted blacksmith's vice was followed by wooden vices. Wood bench screws with a mating wooden nut were factory-produced or tools were available for the craftsman to make his own, usually from beech. A fine or small thread cannot be made in wood, as it would break or crumble, so screws were about $2\frac{1}{2}$in diameter and often about 2ft long. The blank for the screw was turned on a lathe and a

J

skilled worker might 'chase' a thread using a lathe tool free-hand, going deeper with successive cuts. It was more usual to cut it with a tool working like the engineer's die, but made of wood with two cutters, that could be adjusted for a series of deepening cuts. The mating internal thread could be chased freehand in a lathe, but it was more usually cut with a tapered tap. Early teeth started the thread, then as the tap continued in the later teeth, deepened the thread.

The usual woodworker's vice for a long time consisted of a large front jaw sloping sideways and reaching almost to the floor. Movement of the screw was matched by altering the position of a peg through a hole (Fig 24E). The side of the bench formed the inner jaw, but this was usually arranged to have a replaceable section to allow for wear. The use of a peg at the foot meant that the jaw was not always parallel which may have made precision work difficult at some settings. So that withdrawing the screw would bring the jaw with it, a hardwood piece through a mortice in the side of the jaw, engaged with a groove in the neck of the screw (Fig 24F).

A vice of this type, but standing independently on a low stool, is from a wheelwright's shop in Witney and is now in the museum at Woodstock (Fig 24G).

A lighter vice had two screws, without any extension to a pegged piece (Fig 24H), providing a parallel action so long as the work being held passed through between the screws. These lighter screws were also used to make a cramp (possibly of hornbeam for strength in the thread)—one screw pulling the jaws together and the other pushing the end opposite to the grip apart (Fig 24J).

The wooden vice screws were followed by steel ones with square or buttress threads, factory-made. These were used for vices similar to those with wooden screws. The nut part had a flange to fix to a wooden block below the bench. This vice continued until the adoption of the modern parallel-action vice.

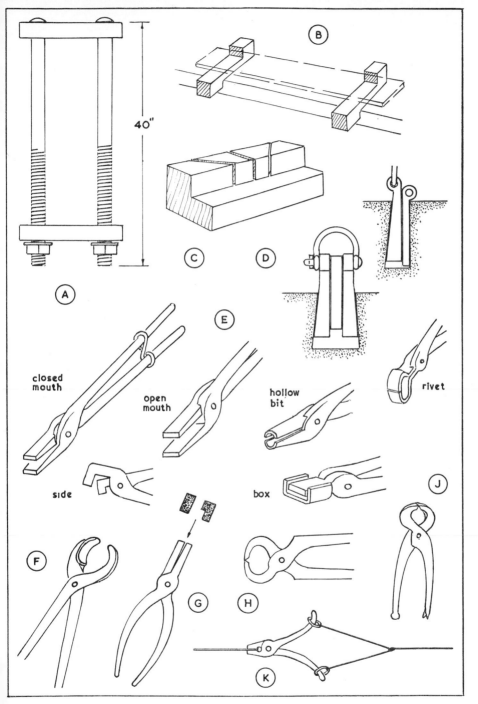

40"

B

C

D

E

closed
mouth

open
mouth

hollow
bit

rivet

A

side

box

J

F

G

H

K

Fig 25 Work guides, tongs and pincers

There have been examples of wooden G cramps, using wooden screws and having the parts tenonned together, but these were not very successful. Iron G cramps, similar to modern ones, were made by the smith. As they were few, they tended to be large, and smaller jobs were accommodated with packings.

The wheelwright's 'Samson' was a heavy cramp with two screws, used for tightening the felloes as the wheel was assembled (Fig 25A).

For sawing wood on the bench, bench hooks were used, often in pairs (Fig 25B). These were narrow and cut from solid wood. The wider single bench hook seems to be more recent. If built up, the parts were held by glued dowels instead of nails or screws, so that there was no metal to blunt a saw. A bench hook was also used as a shooting board for end grain, with a low-angle plane on edge. Cutting back one crossbar so that the saw did not drop through and mark the bench seems to be a modern idea. A mitre block (Fig 25C), cut from the solid or built up, was used by woodworkers with any sort of framing to do. This was held in the vice or made to be used like a bench hook.

Stonemasons used 'nippers' similar to the 'lazy tongs' of the woodman (Fig 23E). For a more positive lift, with stone too heavy or unsuitable for nippers, a hole was chopped out and a 'lewis' used. There were variations, but the grip was provided by a wedge or dovetail action inside the hole (Fig 25D). The hole was made wider at the bottom, then one or two tapered pieces inserted and a removable filler piece forced the tapered pieces to the sides of the hole.

The tongs or plier principle has been known for a long time and was probably introduced by the smith in earlier civilisations. He made his own tools and needed many tongs to hold hot metal. A smith's tongs have long handles and short jaws to give considerable leverage. For thin work the jaws meet when closed, but 'open-mouth' tongs do not meet and give a grip nearer parallel on thicker work. There are a great variety of shapes of

142

tongs and the smith tends to make new ones to suit particular jobs (Fig 25E). They could be locked on a job by a loop or figure-eight piece of metal slipped over the handles.

The smith also made tongs for other craftsmen. The wheelwright used tongs with special jaws for holding and levering spokes when assembling them to the felloes (Fig 25F). Some basketmakers had a similar tool for bending rods, and called it a 'commander', but others used this name for a handled weight, used for hitting. Another basketmaking tool had one flat jaw and one L-shaped, which was used for bruising and kinking cane to bend it (Fig 25G).

Pincers have been known for a long time—not always for withdrawing nails; they are pictured as instruments of torture in the Middle Ages. The broad end to give leverage was usual (Fig 25H), but what became known as 'Lancashire' pincers were without the shoulder (Fig 25J). Small tongs preceded pliers, which do not have such a long history. Pliers for more delicate work were used by town craftsmen, working in silver and other precious metals. Some other pliers may have found their way into the country, while after the Industrial Revolution pliers were quantity-produced. Pliers with their ends turned out, so that a pull tightened them, were used for wire drawing (Fig 25K).

Workers in leather and fabrics used tongs or pliers with broad jaws, so as to spread the strain in fixing upholstery. Metalworkers used a miniature version of the smith's vice as a hand vice for holding small work.

CHAPTER 10

Measuring and Marking Out

Anyone concerned with making or repairing anything is constantly referring to a rule or tape measure, yet in the not very distant past a craftsman would go through most of his working day without using any such measuring device. Measurement in the sense of feet and inches, metric measure or other system, does not matter until parts which are made in different places have to be compared or brought together to be fitted. Only then is it convenient to be able to quote positive sizes related to some standard of measurement. Where the craftsman made a complete product by his own hands, he could try parts against each other and fit one to another as his work progressed. It did not matter if what he was making was bigger or smaller than a similar thing made by someone else. Even with more precise things like screw threads, providing the nut fitted the bolt it did not have to be made to any laid-down standard.

Because craftsmen in one place had little need to refer sizes to craftsmen in other places, units of measurement to the degree of accuracy expected today did not become stabilised until the Industrial Revolution. Coupled with the lack of need of accurate measuring devices was the fact that many craftsmen could not read or write and might not even have been familiar with normal figures. Counting in fives was common. It could be done on

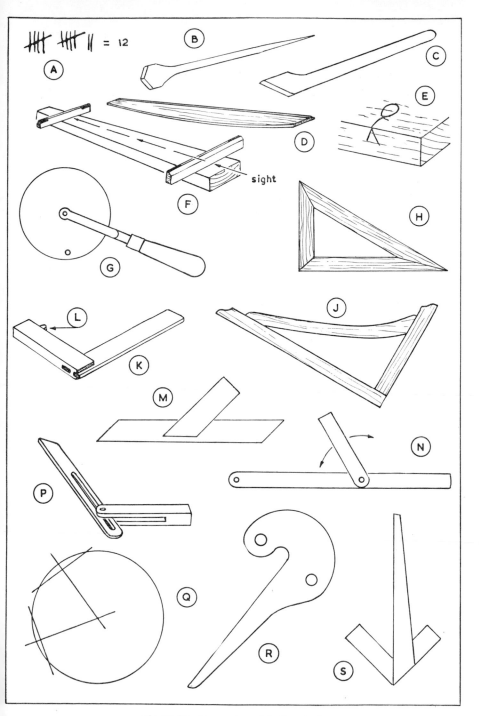

Fig 26 Marking-out and testing tools

a hand and written by making a stroke for each one, with a stroke across at each fifth to indicate the completion of a group (Fig 26A). This is still convenient and is sometimes seen where objects have to be counted—as in poles in a pile or animals passing a point.

Gauges were used where items had to be compared or made the same size. Notching the end of a piece of wood was common. Pencils and similar marking devices were uncommon, but there was always a cutting tool to make a notch. For such things as slates, where stock sizes had to be produced, the measuring tool was a 'wippet stick' with notches in it. A size of slate had a particular local name and this was shown on the stick by a symbol rather than a figure. Additional measuring sticks for other workers were made by reference to the first and not by measuring with a rule, as we should today.

For pieces like the many shaped parts of a cart, there were templates, which had been altered or corrected over the production of many vehicles, until the shape and size were known to be right for the purpose. Then, if a farmer wanted a variation, this could be incorporated by indicating 'the width of a hand more' or something like that, without reference to feet and inches.

Of course, inches and feet were known and used, and a craftsman would have a marked rule, but its accuracy in relation to similar marked rules in other parts of the country would be doubtful until the coming of machine-divided factory-produced tools.

The first attempt to standardise measurements was said to be by King Alfred, the first king of all England, who produced standard measuring rods, weights and grain measures, for other equipment to be checked against. In 1305 King Edward I decreed that 'three grains of barley, dry and round, make an inch; twelve inches make a foot; three feet make an ulna, five and a half ulnas make a rod; and forty rods in length and breadth make an acre'. The word 'ulna' gave way to 'yard', but these sizes persisted and we are only now changing to more logical ways of measuring.

An inch was supposed to be the length of a finger joint, a foot was the length of a man's foot and a yard was the length of his stride—all things liable to wide variations, so they could only be treated as approximations. Larger measures might be based on the amount of work which could be done by a team of horses in a given time, and similar variables; hence the often peculiar British measurements.

When railway pioneers were looking for a width between rails to adopt as a standard, they settled on the track of cart ruts in a local lane. Obviously the width between wheels of all carts in an area had to be made the same, otherwise they would have been in difficulty with the deeply-rutted unmade local roads. This is still the standard British track and is used in many countries of the world. By measurement, it is 4ft 8½in, but if those early cart makers had been using a rule, we might have had a more logical round number of feet.

Measurements of length were often compared with 'rods', which were straight-edged pieces of wood on which all the vital sizes were marked. The rod was held against the job and the distance marked. Even in modern cabinetmaking it is customary to mark out a rod before starting a piece of furniture and use this for reference rather than go back to a rule or tape measure for each length required. A rod marked in 'hands', with a sliding gauge for measuring heights of horses, was found still in use in a Warwickshire sales yard while preparing this book.

Pencils, as we know them, are fairly recent. Lead or chalk might be used, but a scratch or cut was more accurate for marking out wood. A pointed awl can mark the centres of holes or scratch lines, but a marking knife is better. A general-purpose knife may have been used, but a piece of steel with an awl point at one end could have a single or double cutting edge at the other end (Fig 26B). A broad single-bladed marking knife was known as a 'London' marking knife (Fig 26C).

A craftsman made his own straight-edge for drawing lines or checking surfaces, from straight-grained well-seasoned hardwood (Fig 26D). More often, the careful worker had a pair of straight-edges, so that one could be used to check the other.

For straightness longer than the wooden straight-edge, a taut string was used. This is still the method for checking walling and other work of considerable length. A string may be a 'chalk line' and be used for 'striking' straight lines. The end of the line is held by an assistant or tied to an awl, then it is rubbed with chalk. If it is stretched and the centre lifted slightly and released, it deposits a straight line of chalk. This method was used when setting out full-size drawings on the floor. It is still the recognised way of making long straight lines when 'lofting' the lines for a yacht or ship. It was also the method used for marking the line on the adzed top surface of a log to be cut with a pit saw. The finer the cord, the finer the struck line.

Before the days of machine planing, wood prepared by hand on the bench was first planed to give a true face side, then a face edge planed at right-angles to it. This was marked (Fig 26E) and all other measurements taken from these surfaces. In planing a face side, it was possible to get the wood flat in its width, yet it could be twisted in its length. It was said to be 'in winding', which might have been seen by sighting along, but it was more easily checked by viewing along a pair of identical straight-edges, called 'winding strips' (Fig 26F). Contrasting coloured woods were let into the edges and there might be pegs mating with holes, so that the strips could be stored together.

The wheelwright and his smith used a 'traveller' (Fig 26G) to compare the distance around the wheel rim and its iron tyre, without reference to feet and inches, by counting the revolutions as a mark or hole near the circumference of the wheel passed the handle as it was rolled around the job. Similar tools were used for measuring in other crafts, and a more sophisticated version with a recording dial is used today for land measuring.

Most craftsmen needed to be able to mark and check a right-angle. Simplest was a small set-square, either solid, or built up with strips (Fig 26H). The blacksmith and the mason used an L-shaped piece of metal. The long edge of a set-square might have been at another angle required, as in draughtsmen's squares today, but some large set-squares had shaped diagonal pieces (Fig 26J). Other set-squares had stops on their edge to hook over an edge of the job, and these developed into try-squares (Fig 26K). An all-wood try-square had its blade fixed to the stock with a special mortice and tenon joint and a large one had a peg to prevent it tipping (Fig 26L). As the accuracy of a wooden try-square may vary according to the amount of moisture taken up or lost by the wood, it had to be tested occasionally by drawing a line while against a straight edge, then turning over to see if it matched. For picture framing, and similar work, a mitre-square was made with the blade at 45° to the stock and projecting both sides of it (Fig 26M).

For other angles there were adjustable bevels, with two pieces bolted or riveted together so that they could be moved and friction would hold them. A blacksmith had an iron one, with one leg extended to form a handle (Fig 26N). Slotting one or both blades allowed the tool to go into restricted places. Slotting the blade into a stock allowed the tool to be used like a try-square (Fig 26P) and this is the form used today.

For drawing lines at right-angles to a curved edge, or for finding the centre of a circular object, as when locating a lathe centre, the tool used was a 'round-square' or 'centre-square'. This design was based on the fact that a line bisecting a chord of a circle must pass through or point at the centre of the circle (Fig 26Q). One form of round-square has two pegs and the marking

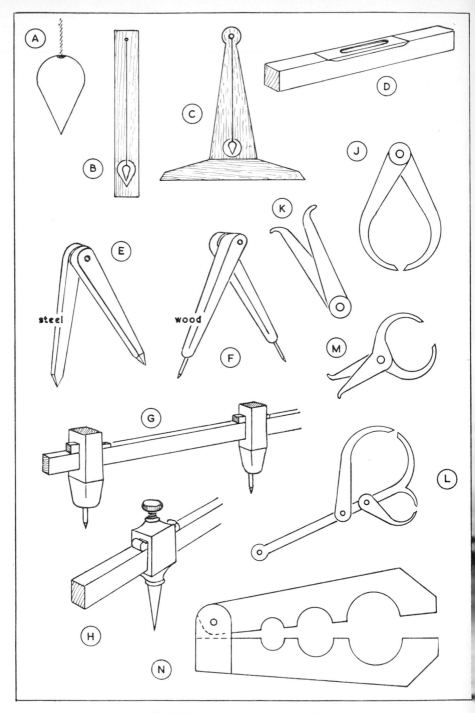

Fig 27 Levels, compasses and calipers

edge at right-angles to them (Fig 26R). This could not be used on a circle smaller than the space between the pegs, but it was useful for large circles, like the rim of a cart wheel. The other type had the marking edge projecting from an L-shaped head (Fig 26S). This was particularly suitable for finding the centres of smaller circles. Lines drawn at two positions crossed at the centre.

A weight on a line used as a means of testing if a thing were vertical seems to have been known from earliest times. Giving the weight ('plumb bob') a point directly below the string, allowed a position to be marked below it which was then exactly under the hanging point of the string (Fig 27A). Mounting the line and bob on a board, produced a plumb rule (Fig 27B) for holding against a surface, such as a wall, to test its verticality. The string was observed against a marked line on the board and the point of the bob in relation to a mark on the hole in which it swung.

The plumb line was also used to check horizontal surfaces, by having another piece at right angles to the plumb rule, either at the top or bottom (Fig 27C). Another test was to observe the level of water in a pan or saucer in relation to a line marked around parallel with the base. However, the spirit level was invented in the seventeenth century and this more precise tool became accepted and is still the recognised tool for checking horizontal surfaces (Fig 27D).

Dividers or compasses also go back into antiquity. Most had two points, and we would call them 'dividers' today, keeping the name 'compass' for a tool with a pencil point, but 'compass' was the general name, even with two points. The blacksmith made iron or steel dividers, possibly with a soft metal washer in the bolted or rivetted joint to help friction (Fig 27E). Wooden tools were also made, with steel points (Fig 27F). Besides drawing circles, compasses were used to compare measurements, and step off equal distances, as with ladder rung spacings.

For distances outside the reach of a compass there were trammels. A wooden version had a pair of heads sliding on a wood bar and locked with wedges (Fig 27G). Points were sharpened nails. By choosing a suitable length of batten, almost any distance could be spanned. Better versions used a cast metal box, with a screw arrangement and a steel point (Fig 27H). This might go on a metal rod, but was more likely to fit a wooden batten up to about $1\frac{1}{2}$in by $\frac{3}{4}$in.

For many centuries, the tool for checking round objects has been the caliper. Basically, calipers were made like compasses, with curved legs for outside curves (Fig 27J) and straight outward pointing legs for inside curves (Fig 27K). A smith made his with a long handle, and might have large and small calipers on the same handle (Fig 27L). Wooden calipers were made like wooden compasses, with bent steel points. Combination calipers were made to show the same inside and outside sizes (Fig 27M). Screw adjusting calipers and compasses are modern developments originating in America. Sliding calipers were used by smiths. Modern versions of these are calibrated and have verniers for close measurements. Modern engineers' micrometers are developments of the basic caliper.

Turners in wood and metal made considerable use of calipers, but they had their own gauges. A block of wood with holes of sizes needed could be used to test turned parts. Better than this was a hinged gauge, with half of each hole in each piece (Fig 27N).

Most craftsmen in solid materials had a need to mark lines parallel with an edge. One tool for doing this was a variation on the caliper, with one pointed leg (Fig 28A), called a 'jenny' caliper in Britain and a 'hermaphrodite' caliper in America. With the hooked leg against an edge, the point could be made to scratch a line parallel to the edge, when the tool was drawn along.

The woodworker had his gauge for marking lines parallel

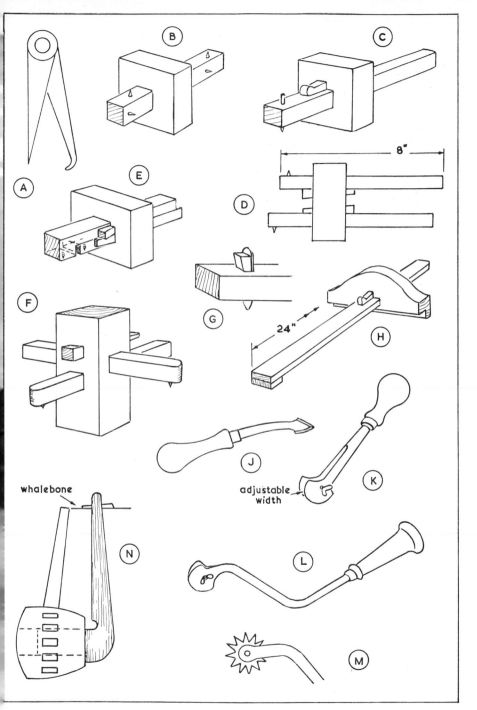

Fig 28 Gauges for woodwork and leatherwork

with an edge and there have been many ingenious variations on this. Basically, there is a head to bear against an edge, while a stock with a marking point passes through it. Where standard distances were required frequently the stock could be fixed in the head and up to eight fixed distances could be used, by driving in nails and filing their ends to make points (Fig 28B).

In an adjustable gauge the stock slides through the head. A popular type had the stock held where required by a wedge (Fig 28C). The more recent gauge of this type had a screw to hold the beech or rosewood stock, and many gauges produced had boxwood screws. These are only now giving way to plastic.

It is sometimes convenient to be able to have a gauge with two settings. A Swedish example has two wedge-controlled stocks on opposite sides, all made from hornbeam (Fig 28D). This could be used to mark the two sides of mortices and tenons. With the two points the same way, both sides would be marked at the same time (Fig 28E). Another gauge with two stocks was arranged so that both could be locked with one wedge (Fig 28F). Modern mortice gauges have two points the same way, but with factory-made brass screws and slides.

Some much-used marking gauges had their heads faced with brass to prevent wear. The normal marking gauge scratches. For work across the grain it is better to cut. A cutting gauge had a small knife, held by a wedge (Fig 28G). Besides marking across the grain, this could be used for cutting parallel strips of thin wood or veneer.

While lines further than a few inches from an edge could be drawn by measuring, trying to do it with an ordinary marking gauge having a head less than 3in across would be difficult as the gauge would wobble. Some craftsmen made a panel gauge (Fig 28H). The head had a rebate to run on the edge of the panel being marked and the fairly substantial stock was held by a wedge. One hand controlled the head while the other pressed the point.

154

Page 156 A pole lathe at the Forestry Commission Mayswood Centre

Leatherworkers had a use for a cutting gauge similar to the woodworker's for cutting strips parallel to an edge. Marking on leather can be done with a blunt rounded knife blade as this leaves a dark brown line. The basic saddler's marking tool was called a single 'crease' (Fig 28J). Heating it would make a more definite mark. A screw crease (Fig 28K) works in the same way as a jenny caliper—one point overlaps the edge and acts as a guide, while the other marks the surface. The screw allows adjustment of width. The small crease, or checker, was held in the hand, but for heavy work there was a 'shoulder crease' (Fig 28L), long enough to put the shoulder against. Tools of similar construction, but with patterned points, were used for decoration. 'Prick wheels' were used for marking stitch holes (Fig 28M) or this would be done with a stitch punch or pricking iron (Fig 20Q). In both cases a separate tool was needed for each stitch spacing.

Gauges were used to check assemblies. The wheelwright's greatest need for accuracy came in the assembly of a wheel, which had to run true, despite its size and apparent clumsiness. Spokes had to be set up in the hub so that they were all at the same angle to the axle line, to give the correct 'dish' to the wheel. With the wheel supported on a double trestle ('morticing cradle'), or over a long narrow pit, if it were a very large wheel, a spoke-set gauge was fitted into the hub (Fig 28N). Details of design varied, but basically a close-fitting stub rotated in the axle hole and an arm carried a light gauge to check the spoke angle. To give the required sensitivity, the contact was a piece of whalebone held by a wedge. A millwright used a rather similar device to check the surface of a mill wheel in relation to the post on which it turned.

As better communications came about with improved roads and the coming of canals and railways, craftsmen ceased to be isolated and factory-made items came into use, so that measurements to give greater accuracy and take care of interchange-

K

ability became more important. In early Victorian days, and maybe before that, accurate rules became more important. Woodworking craftsmen favoured a fourfold 2ft or 3ft rule, often made of boxwood with brass joints. The apparently clumsy rule was not usually marked less than 1/16in and had to be stood on edge to bring the graduations near to the working surface. This could be carried in an apron pocket. For bench use there were rules, made of similar material, but without joints, although not usually stout enough to be trusted as straight-edges.

Metalworkers favoured a 2ft steel rule with only a centre joint, which had a catch to hold the opened rule straight. Finer graduations reflected the greater precision possible in metal. As hot metal would take the temper from a steel rule, there were brass versions made for use by blacksmiths. Engineers' bench rules were without joints and could be used as straight-edges.

CHAPTER 11

Turning and Round Work

A round article can be fashioned by rotating the material and holding a tool against it, or the work may be stationary while some sort of rounding device is revolved on it. The latter method has its uses for poles or tapered ends of rungs, but anything more intricate is made by revolving the work in a lathe. Making articles on a lathe has been known as 'turning' and the products as 'turnery', but these names were also used in Wales for carved spoons and similar things as well, presumably because they were often the products of the man who also made things on a lathe.

The technique of shaping something by holding a tool against it while it is rotated goes back into antiquity and must have come about not long after the discovery of the wheel. There is mention by Pliny of Theodor, of Samas, as being the probable inventor in 740BC. The potter's wheel for shaping clay is a form of lathe and this probably came before the use of the principle for shaping harder and more solid materials. The rotating fire stick may have also shown the way, and methods of getting more power into the spinning of this would have provided ideas for the making and driving of primitive lathes.

It is in the method of rotating the work that turning equipment has shown the greatest variations. A piece of wood sup-

Fig 29 Wood-turning lathes and tools

ported on two points might be spun by hand, but the speed would obviously be very slow and the labour considerable. Wrapping a strap or cord around the work allows two helpers to pull backwards and forwards and build up a good speed (Fig 29A). Attaching the strap to a bow, in the manner of a fire drill, allowed the rotating to be done by one man (Fig 29B). In India craftsmen still use lathes of this type. They are near floor level and are driven by the operator, who sits on the ground, working the bow with one hand and using a foot to assist the other hand in controlling the tool.

British pole lathes used the same reciprocating principle. A springy bough had a cord looped around the job and the worker's foot provided the downward pressure, while the bough above took care of the return. In its simplest form the worker's foot was in a loop in the cord (Fig 29C), but most of these lathes had a treadle. Despite the coming of mechanisation, these lathes have persisted in use until recent times. Chair bodgers, working in the woods around High Wycombe, set up their pole lathes and produced chair legs, stretchers and rails by this means until after the last war. One of the last professional users of a pole lathe was George Lailey of Bucklebury, near Reading, who died in 1958 and was turning bowls almost until his death, carrying on a business which had been there amongst other rural crafts for at least 200 years. His lathe and equipment are now in the University of Reading Museum of English Rural Life.

One reason for the continuing use of pole lathes was the ease with which they could be set up from materials found mostly on the spot. When the supply of chair wood in the immediate area was exhausted, a large machine did not have to be transported, but a few vital pieces could be taken to build into a new lathe made elsewhere. The pole was a length of alder or other wood, chosen with the right degree of springiness—too stiff a pole made hard work of treadling and too whippy a pole might not keep sufficient grip on the cord around the work or return the cord smartly enough. The pole length had to be 12ft or so, and it had to be arranged anchored outside the shelter around the lathe.

The lathe bed consisted of two stout and reasonably straight pieces, fixed to equally stout posts driven into the ground and braced with struts, if necessary. The lathe needed to stand firm. One head could have been an extended post, but most pole lathes had both heads movable on the bed and usually held by wedges (Fig 29D). In modern parlance, these formed the 'head-stock' and 'tailstock', but were variously called 'heads', 'centres' or 'poppets'. For turning chair rails and legs, both centres on which the work rotated were steel. In the better lathes, one centre had a screw adjustment to allow easy changing of work without altering the wedges (Fig 29E). The drive was provided by the cord passing directly around the work. This could be the rope or cord itself, or a piece of leather strap included to increase friction (Fig 29F). The work height was not much above waist level for chair bodging, but some bowl turners preferred the centre of the work almost at shoulder level.

A bowl turner favoured the tailstock centre bent on the top of the wood support, so as to give the minimum interference with his tool movement (Fig 29G). As the drive could not be taken around the bowl, there was a mandrel, put between the tail centre and the job to take the strap drive and transfer it to the bowl. The larger diameter of a bowl meant that there was considerable strain on the drive when the outside was being turned. One method of transferring the drive used four chisel-like ends (Fig 29H) pressed into the job.

The treadle was usually quite crude and arranged to pull the cord on the opposite side from the worker. A cut was made on the wood when the top of the job was rotating towards the worker's left side. As the turner had to stand on one foot to use the treadle, he sometimes arranged a rail to lean against in a semi-sitting posture. A man needed to be on his feet to exert sufficient power. Long lathes were sometimes made for turning such things as broom handles with the treadle arranged lengthwise.

The tool had to rest against something and this was usually a piece of wood notched into the support (Fig 29J) or arranged on other parts of the structure of the lathe or hut.

Another, but much less common way of providing a similar drive used a bow above the lathe (Fig 29K). This avoided having to arrange a pole extending a long way outside the shelter.

A snag with the driving methods so far covered is that the work reciprocates—having to rotate a similar amount both ways, yet a cut can only be made one way; the downstroke of the treadle. A traditional turner became extremely skilful with this type of lathe, but it is obviously more efficient to have the work rotating in the cutting direction all the time. A handle directly on the end of the work could not give a high enough speed, so a pulley drive from a large to a small wheel was needed. The wheelwright used this method for turning wheel hubs on a massive wooden lathe, the power coming from a large wheel, made like a cart wheel and with a handle for two men to turn.

Treadle lathes, with a flywheel to maintain speed and rotation, came into use in the eighteenth century or before, and these were used for more precise wood turning and some metal turning, but more by town craftsmen than by rural workers. Lathes, as used by the wheelwright, were also employed in other crafts when the size of the work was more than could be treadled. These were called 'throw lathes' and the driving wheel, at which two men would have to work hard, might be some way from the lathe, with a belt drive to a small pulley on the lathe. Of course, the coming of steam, gas and electric power transformed this.

Turning is easier if the work is rotating quickly. Surface finish is better. Shapes are more easily obtained. Heavier cuts may be taken without risk of digging the tool in and tearing the grain. Modern power-driven lathes are very much faster than was possible by man-power. Consequently, traditional work may not have had the finish of modern turning and would have taken longer, but an experienced man could produce an acceptable finish in a reasonable time—and had to if he were to make a living.

Wood was prepared as closely as possible to the intended sizes by froe and axe, usually to a roughly octagonal section, so as to reduce the amount of turning tool work needed. Wood for chair legs and rails might be turned without having allowed much time for seasoning. Wood for bowls and similar things had to be left to season after roughing to shape and before putting in the lathe.

There were two basic tools for external turning. Although modern factory-produced tools have long blades, blacksmith-made tools tended to be much shorter. In any case a lathe tool was given a long wooden handle, to provide leverage. For roughing to shape there were gouges in several widths, sharpened with outside bevels and the ends rounded (Fig 29L). These were pointed directly at the work and cut with a scraping action that left a rough surface. The work was taken down to final size and a smooth surface given by using a chisel, sharpened both sides and with a skew end, so that it could be used with a slicing action (Fig 29M). Chisels were used in many widths. Few other tools were needed for external work, but a parting tool (Fig 29N) would separate parts with the minimum of waste and some workers had a chisel bevelled both ways (Fig 29P). Although the bead on chair legs could be made with a chisel, some craftsmen used a V-tool, similar to that used by a carver, probably for greater speed in production.

Sycamore was chosen for bowls and similar objects for use with food. This wood was fairly plentiful in Wales, where bowls were made individually—one from each block of wood. In some other parts of Britain elm was used for bowls and craftsmen devised special tools which allowed them to turn one bowl inside another. These were curved to follow the bowl shape and had sharpened ends, usually hook-shaped (Fig 29Q). Inner bowls had to be split from the outer one and could not be given as good a finish on the lathe, so there had to be some benchwork afterwards, but the technique allowed several bowls to be produced from what would otherwise have disappeared in shavings. Some inner curves cannot be worked with gouge and chisel. For these jobs the turner made scraping tools (Fig 29R) from old files.

In a lathe where there was a pulley in the headstock, the drive was transmitted to the work by a centre with spurs, a common one being similar to that used today (Fig 29S). For small things, such as eggcups, there was a screw centre (Fig 29T). Some work was merely held by friction in a wood block (Fig 29U). The square tops of table legs provided a positive drive in a hole (Fig 29V).

Metal turning never was a country craft, except that the wood turners might make ferrules for handles. For turning the end of brass tubes, he used a square-section tool sharpened to a diamond-shape cutting edge (Fig 29W). An engineer's lathe only found its way into the blacksmith's shop when he had to broaden his scope to deal with the more technical requirements being introduced to farming in this century.

While a lathe is the obvious tool for producing round articles, some other tools were used. Wooden dowels were made by driving through a steel plate (Fig 13K), while rake tines were rounded by driving through a tubular cutter (Fig 13L).

Long round rods, such as handles for various tools like rakes and brooms, could be held in a brake and shaped from natural poles by a tool which had many names, including 'stail engine', 'engine', 'rounder', 'nug', 'nog' and 'pole shave'. As these were individually made, there were several variations in design. The tool functions like a pencil sharpener. In its simplest form there

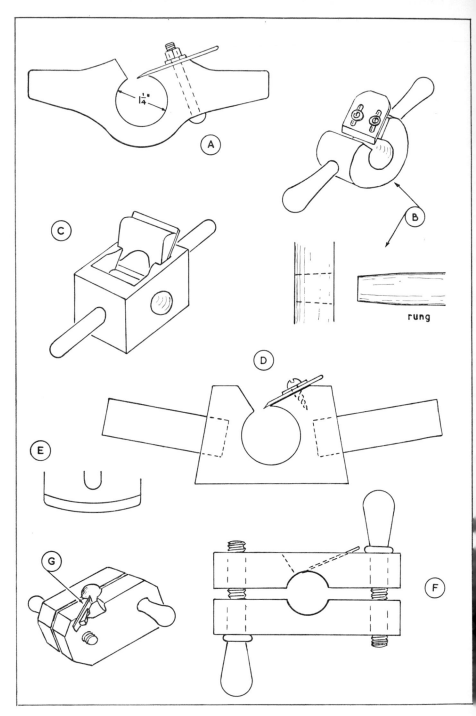

rung

Fig 30 Rounding tools

is a hole with a slight taper through a block of wood and a cutter (an old plane iron) fixed so as to pare the wood as the tool is rotated and moved along the rod (Fig 30A). A simple 'rung engine', like this, with a hole of a size and taper to match a shell bit or tapered auger, could taper the end of a ladder rung quickly and accurately (Fig 30B).

For working along a pole, a thick stail engine would keep in line easier than a thinner tool. Hole sizes were about $1\frac{1}{4}$in for long tool handles. The cutter had to be arranged so as to slice around the circumference. In some cases it was wedged like a plane iron (Fig 30C). More often an old plane iron, worn almost to the limit, was held by a bolt or screw (Fig 30D). Sharpening the edge to a curve prevented digging in (Fig 30E).

A better tool was made in two parts with wooden screws to provide adjustment so as to cover a small range of sizes (Fig 30F). Some had two blades—one in each part. A further refinement was to give the tool a second narrow or curved cutter, which worked ahead of the main one and removed bark before the main cutter trued the wood (Fig 30G). An adjustable stail engine could be made to work a taper, by altering its setting as it progressed.

CHAPTER 12

Rural Engineering

Until the coming of the internal combustion engine and the consequent development of garages to service motor cars the only rural metalworker was the blacksmith. He had to be versatile. While he might have to operate as a farrier, shoeing horses for much of his time, he would also be called on to make tools for other crafts, make the fittings for waggons and other equipment, produce and repair armour, and deal with domestic pots and pans.

The smithy was the centre of interest in every medieval village and the smith's trade goes back into antiquity. Horse-shoeing was added to his activities in Roman times. It would only be in the last few centuries that he would have been called a 'blacksmith' to distinguish him from the 'whitesmith', who dealt with plumbing, tinsmithing and associated work.

The smith's tools have varied less throughout history than those of many other trades. Tools used today to do work by hand and hot metal would be recognised and understood by a smith of many centuries ago, or even of Biblical times. The smith's trade enabled him to make many of his own tools, so there were individual variations, but there was a general similarity between tools used by smiths in widely scattered places. Some of the smith's tools—holding devices, measuring tools and

168

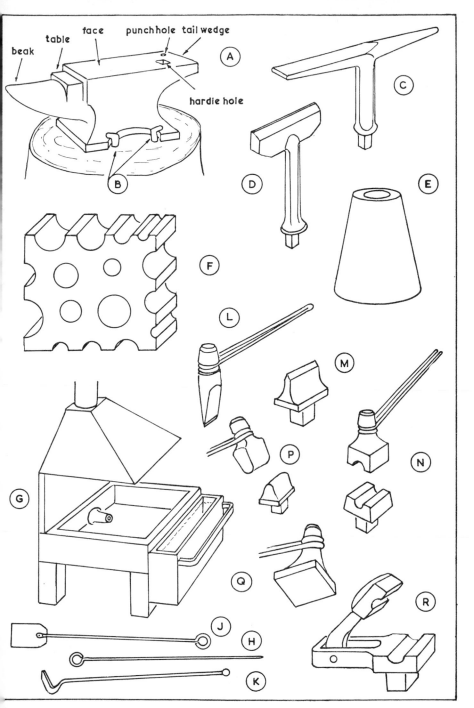

Fig 31 Blacksmiths' tools

the means of making holes—have been described in other sections. Tools covered in this chapter are peculiar to other processes in smithing.

The centre of most activity in the smithy was the anvil. Sizes and shapes varied, being anywhere between 56lb and over 2cwt, with overall lengths between 15in and 30in. The village smith used the largest of these. Smaller anvils were for specialist trades, like nail and chain making. Anvils are now cast steel, but earlier ones were wrought or cast iron, with a steel face. Anvils have been made in many forms, and there are examples with two beaks, but the general shape favoured in Britain and elsewhere became settled in the thirteenth century. Many earlier anvils were without beaks.

Most work was done on the face, which was slightly rounded, but cutting or chopping was done on the softer surface of the 'table' ('step' or 'block'), which was stepped down from the face, between it and the 'beak' ('bick' or 'horn'). This avoided damaging the face with cutting tools and of blunting tools on a hardened face. On most anvils there was a square hole in the 'tail wedge' ('hanging end') to accept bottom tools, and a round hole that allowed metal to be punched through (Fig 31A).

There are cast iron anvil stands, with tops recessed to locate the anvil, but these do not provide any cushioning to blows and are noisy. The smith favoured a section of oak or elm tree trunk set in the smithy floor. This gave 'life' to hammer blows, was resilient and deadened noise. The usual anvil had no holes in the base, but was held down by spikes which the smith made to hook over the feet (Fig 31B).

The anvil was necessarily massive to withstand heavy work being done on it. For more delicate work the smith had tools to fit the square hole in the anvil or mount in its own tree trunk. These had the general name of 'stakes'. A 'bick iron' gave the same sort of faces as an anvil, but for finer work (Fig 31C). A 'hatchet stake' was more of a tinsmith's tool, but it gave a straight edge over which sheet metal could be folded (Fig 31D) A 'half moon stake' was similar to a hatchet stake, but with a curved edge.

If the smith's work involved assembling or making parts which had to be flat, as in building up an ornamental gate, he had a large thick iron slab with a flat top, called a 'levelling plate'. If the work involved shaping rings, he had a conical cast iron 'floor mandrel' on which they could be hammered or pressed to true circles (Fig 31E). For varied work, particularly if the smithy was associated with a wheelwright shop, the smith had several mandrels in sizes from about 12in for hub bands up to 4ft to suit wheel tyres.

The smith had a 'swage block' (Fig 31F) for shaping curved and V-shaped pieces. This was a large cast block, with hollows and holes of many sizes, so that a range of different curves and other forms could be accurately shaped and a series of curved parts made to match. The block was moved around to present the correct side upwards and was usually mounted on a block to bring it to a convenient working height.

The intense heat for forgework has been obtained by the use of bellows of many sorts from as far back as the smith's work can be traced. The Egyptians used a pair of goatskins, which were stood on and pressed alternately. In the East, Chuka bellows were hand-operated triangular skin bags with pottery nozzles. Huza bellows were goatskin bags, held in the hand and with wood lips as inlet valves, which closed as the fist was clenched. The Lakhers smiths, of Tibet, used similar hand bellows, with a pair of vertical bamboo pieces as cylinders and cane plungers with cloth or feather on the end as pistons.

British, American and most European smiths used bellows which were nearly always double-acting. Some were shaped like larger versions of domestic bellows, with wooden pieces having flexible leather sides. Leather flaps acted as valves to let air into alternate sides, as one half blew and the other half filled. A similar action was used with the two halves round and mounted in a frame. Weights were used to increase pressure, and the operation was by a lever projecting to a position where an assistant could tend the fire and work the bellows. As a considerable amount of air was needed to build up sufficient heat, the bellows might be 6ft or so across and occupy a large part of the smithy. Bellows have given way to fan blowers, usually power-driven.

The hearth or forge was built of stone, brick or cast iron, with a water trough (called a 'boshe' in some parts of Britain) built in or arranged alongside. Air from the bellows entered through a nozzle called a 'tue iron' (pronounced 'twee iron') (Fig 31G). This might have been solid cast iron, but in constant use its end would burn away in the intense heat and its life was not long. A better tue iron was water jacketted. A 'stop poker' was used to plug the hole in the tue iron and prevent fire being sucked back into some types of bellows, which had to be filled with air.

Fuel was wood, coal or coke. The fire was managed with three tools: a straight or hooked poker (Fig 31H), a flat spade-like slice (Fig 31J) and a rake (Fig 31K). Most work was held with tongs (Fig 25) and all of those in general use were kept on a rack near the hearth, probably on the side of the water trough.

Hot metal was cut in two ways. A 'hot chisel' or 'hot sate' ('sett') could be hit into it (Fig 31L). For cutting cold metal there was a 'cold sate'. This differed in having a more obtuse cutting edge. Light iron or mild steel strips could be cut cold with an edge sharpened to about 60°, while hot metal could be penetrated with an angle not much more than half that. The alternative was to hit the metal on a 'hardie' ('hardy' or 'anvil cutter') (Fig 31M). This was a chisel, mounted in the square hole (often called a 'hardie hole', despite its many other uses) on the anvil. The metal was hammered from both sides until the hardie almost cut through, then the metal was broken off.

172

The tool used like a hardie for cutting bar for horse shoes was called a 'heel cropper'. Bars up to $1\frac{1}{2}$in by $\frac{5}{8}$in for cart horse shoes were cut in this way.

Top and bottom 'swages' (Fig 31N), in many sizes, were used to true hot iron to a round section. Top and bottom 'fullers', in matched sizes, were used to draw down as well as hollow metal (Fig 31P). The action of squeezing the metal as the top fuller was hammered above the first stretched it in the direction of the curve and could be worked along a piece of metal to thin it.

A 'set hammer' and the similar broader 'flatter' (Fig 31Q) were used for hitting with more precision than was possible with a swinging hammer. The flatter, placed over the work, could be hit to flatten the surface and obscure the marks from the hammer or other tool. An 'anvil stake' or 'bottom flatter' was a similar tool which was mounted in the hardie hole.

Most smithing requires the services of a mate. The farrier's mate was his 'doorman'. With an understanding between the pair, the smith holding the work and a hand hammer was able to indicate with taps of the hammer what he wanted the mate to do, usually with a sledge hammer, so that as much as possible could be done with each heating of the metal. One way of doing a job without a mate is seen in an American hinged pair of swages (Fig 31Q).

The fine handled punch for making holes in a horse shoe was called a 'pritchell'. In more recent times nail-making was a specialised trade and a smith bought them readymade but, where nails were made for horse-shoeing, the heads were formed by hammering the redhot end in a 'heading tool' (Fig 32A). If the smith dealt with wrought iron railings and gates, he made several special tools so as to form uniform shapes. A leaf tool (Fig 32B) was a forked iron stake, used with a light leaf hammer (Fig 32C). This combination made decorative leaves, usually at the end of scrolls. For matching scrolls he made a scroll tool (Fig 32D) to pull the hot metal around. A 'monkey tool' was a

L

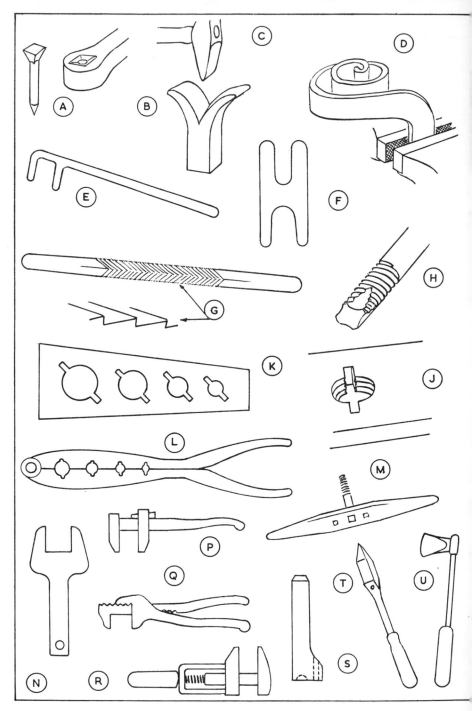

Fig 32 Engineering tools

block of iron with a hole for squaring the shoulders of tenons in gate construction. Another block of iron with a rounded top and hollowed side was called 'snub end scroll' and used for finishing a strip of iron with a rounded tip.

Some wrought ironwork tools were mounted in the hardie hole of the anvil, but others were given their own base to mount on a tree trunk stand. 'Scroll wrenches' or 'dogs' of various sizes were used to pull strip metal to curves (Fig 32E). A 'scroll horn' or 'fork' (Fig 32F) did the same job, but was mounted in a vice and the strip metal worked through it. There is evidence that wrought ironwork was done in the Forest of Dean about 300BC.

Files and rasps were not very efficient hand-made tools until the coming of factory-made tools in the Industrial Revolution. Teeth were raised with a cold chisel, so there was unevenness in the spacing and heights of teeth. The usual arrangement was in what is now called 'single-cut' (Fig 32G). Examples still existing are mostly long square bars, with teeth cut on all four sides and both ends rounded to form handles. These were used by two men to level a horse's hoof or remove scale from forged iron. They would not be very efficient at removing much metal. Finer files for saw sharpening and similar more precise work were mostly the products of specialist makers and comparatively rare in a country workshop.

A square piece, with teeth cut like a file, was called a 'drift' and driven through a hole to true it to a square shape. The same name was given to a tapered round piece used to true round holes or pull holes into line.

Screwcutting with any degree of precision was difficult or impossible in a country workshop until the early nineteenth century. While screws were understood, at least from the times of Archimedes, the means of applying screw action in nut and bolt form was limited by the lack of screwing equipment. A large external thread could be chased by a skilled man on a lathe, in wood or brass, but doing it by hand in steel to make a tap would be impossible. Proper screwcutting lathes in the present form are comparatively recent.

The first 'tap' of a particular size could have its thread filed carefully. Its end was given a slight taper and cutting edges made by filing flats or hollows (Fig 32H). This could be hardened and tempered, then screwed through a hole in a plate, to cut a thread in it. Grooves filed in this made cutting edges, and the plate was hardened and tempered to make a die (Fig 32J). Threads in the die were likely to be more even in pitch than in the handmade tap, as inequalities would even out. The die could then be used to cut a thread on another steel rod to make another tap of greater accuracy. With some handwork as well and possibly further making of taps and dies before satisfaction is reached, a pair of matching tools to produce nuts and bolts could be made. It is understandable that screw threads were avoided, and much use was made of wedges and rivets where screws would be used today. The screw plate, with several sizes of thread in each plate, was the usual means of making external threads (Fig 32K) until the coming of modern dies. One example of an opening type was made like pliers (Fig 32L). This had the advantage of allowing easier access to the cutting edges for touching up.

Taps depended on flats or slight hollows as cutting edges and were turned by a square end in a wrench (Fig 32M).

As there were no standard sizes, nuts were usually roughly squared pieces as chopped by the smith. Consequently there were no standard spanners. The smith forged spanners to suit the nuts and might supply a spanner individually-made with equipment he produced for a customer (Fig 32N). This lack of standardisation also meant that adjustable spanners or wrenches were in demand. One with a sliding jaw, from about 1800, had a wedge for locking (Fig 32P). A later example used a plier action to engage racks (Fig 32Q). A screw-action wrench, of about 1860, showed a move towards the modern shifting spanner (Fig 32R). Pliers or tongs, with the jaws shaped to fit nuts, were also used as spanners.

Riveting as a means of joining metal was much used. Heads were made by hammering, but to true their shape a 'rivet sett' (Fig 32S) was used. A hole in the sett could be slipped over the end of the rivet before hammering, to push sheet metal parts close together.

A blacksmith joined iron by welding—raising the parts almost to melting heat, then hammering them together. Soldering, as a means of joining metal parts, was also understood. Common solder is an alloy of tin and lead, which has a low melting point and an affinity with many other metals. With the use of tinplate in the nineteenth century there was much need of soldering by itinerant tinsmiths repairing and making household articles. A 'soldering iron' had its bit made of copper, which is a good conductor of heat (Fig 32T). It was heated in a flame and used to melt and draw solder along a joint with the aid of a flux to clean both the bit and the work. A 'hatchet' soldering iron went closer into angles (Fig 32U). 'Hard solder', as distinct from the 'soft solder' of the tinsmith, contained silver and needed a higher temperature to melt it, so was used with a blowlamp and a spirit flame for joints in jewellery and small copper or brass articles.

With increasing mechanisation of agriculture and the widening use of the internal combustion engine bringing better communications, the engineer in the country is now at least as mechanised as any town engineer. A modern agricultural engineer may be carrying on a tradition of good craftsmanship, but his technique, methods and equipment are outside the scope of this book.

CHAPTER 13

Agricultural Hand Tools

Now that good roads and the motor car have made it possible for people to live in the country and work in the town, many residents in villages today know little of what goes on locally, but until quite recent times (at least until the 1939–45 war) almost everyone in a village had his or her activities related to the land, either working directly on it or providing a service for those who did. The specialist craftsman might work a few acres or graze animals on the common. Almost everyone kept a pig or other backgarden livestock. Even the vicar had his glebe land, which he might work himself, and the squire kept his home farm under his own control.

Because everyone had a stake in the land with some understanding of its working, the agricultural worker was often considered to be unskilled and certainly not a craftsman in the sense of the wheelwright or blacksmith. His status was lower and his income, if he were an employed man, at many periods was barely on subsistence level. Despite this he was expected to provide many of his own tools. Working the land, in fact, calls for many of the attributes of craftsmanship and the agricultural worker was entitled to be called something better than 'labourer'.

Primitive man started tilling the land by scraping and break-

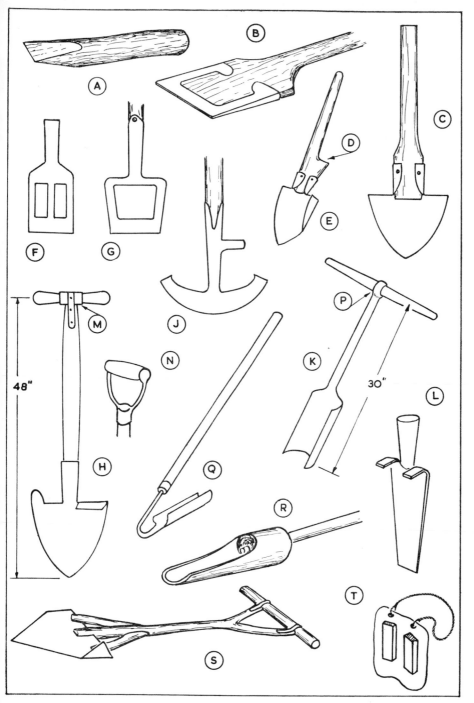

Fig 33 Digging and earthworking tools

ing up the surface with a stick. Some of the earliest recorded tools for tilling soil were wooden sticks arranged to be swung like pick-axes, used by Egyptians about 1500 BC. From this he progressed to a crude plough in which an ox or other animal pulled and the man steered. At first the plough was little more than the scratching stick, possibly tipped with horn or iron, and in India, Iran, Turkey and elsewhere today, ploughs of this sort may still be seen in use.

The alternative to ploughing—and not everyone had the use of a plough—was to dig. There would not seem to be many variations on the spade, but they have been made in many ingenious forms. Simplest is the scratching stick sharpened to a flat form with an axe (Fig 33A). There have been wooden spades made more in the shape of modern tools, but obviously a wooden edge could not dig anything but loose sandy soil and even then might not last long if unprotected. A development had the edge and sides covered in sheet iron (Fig 33B). Large wooden shovels, and spades, without metal edging, were favoured for shovelling grain.

Many iron spades were made from sheet iron. In the simplest form, the metal was wrapped around a handle and nailed on (Fig 33C). The end was either square across or pointed. A variation had a step cut in the handle for the foot (Fig 33D). Turning the edge of the blade stiffened what was a rather weak tool (Fig 33E) and squared the cut, which would be useful when cutting along a line, digging trenches for water courses or for digging peat.

The fork, in the form of a garden digging tool as used today, did not appear to have been very popular, possibly because of the difficulty in making it with adequate strength in the prongs. Instead, there were versions of cutaway spades. For use on heavy land there was an open spade (Fig 33F), rather like a fork with a blade across the end. Brickmakers used another open spade for digging clay (Fig 33G).

A small spade, something like a modern Dutch hoe, was carried by the ploughman for cleaning the plough blade. Some spades had the top turned over to provide a broader surface for the foot. And some workers had a metal or wood plate or 'spud' to tie under their boot to protect it from the top of the spade. One spade with the turned-over top was the 'rutter' spade, a large and heavy tool for cutting drains (Fig 33H). Tools of this type are still used by the Forestry Commission on peat land.

Another variation of the spade was the turf cutter (Fig 33J), something like the smaller tool used today for trimming edges of lawns. A curved spade was used for planting (Fig 33K). This worked something like an auger, cutting a circular plug of soil. A larger version was used for making holes for fence posts. A tapered flat spade cut the sides of square post holes (Fig 33L).

Many spades had handles made of wood from copse or hedgerow and these were often far from straight. The majority of earlier spades had no special grip arranged at the end. While this was satisfactory in soft, loose soils, a T-shaped handle was strapped on with iron (Fig 33M), as the means of making a good mortice and tenon joint was unlikely to be available. Some more comfortable grips were forged by the smith (Fig 33N). For the curved spade, where the handle had to exert considerable turning pressure, an eye was forged in the all-metal tool (Fig 33P).

Before cylindrical drain tiles were introduced, about 1840, heavy land was drained by scooping trenches and using stones or wood to make culverts. A drain scoop (Fig 33Q) was used to scrape out soil from the bottom of the narrow trench. Another tool for a similar purpose was a scoop carved from wood (Fig 33R) and used with a push instead of a pull. Where it was possible to bore a drain hole, as when passing through a bank, shell-type tools similar to those used for hollowing logs were used (Fig 19U).

A heavier type of spade was known as a 'breast plough'. This must have been a very tiring tool to use, as it was pushed by

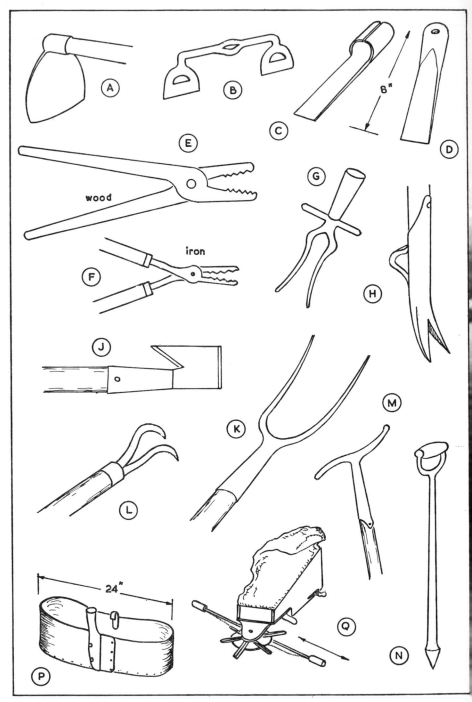

Fig 34 Farmers' tools

leaning against it. Its purpose was to take off turf, where pasture was being turned over to arable. The turf was burned, so that the ash could be used as fertiliser. Versions of the breast plough used a pointed blade, with one edge turned up, fixed to a handle about 5ft long with a large cross handle at the top (Fig 33S). The top might be fixed to a natural crook or something was built up to give stiffness. Construction generally was extremely crude, indicating that the tool was homemade rather than something from a specialist craftsman. Some of the pressure on the chest was relieved by a protector, made with two pieces of wood on a leather apron hung over the shoulders (Fig 33T). Thigh pads were used for a lower thrust.

Hoes do not show much variation. The normal hoe was made like a mattock or adze (Fig 34A). There is a double hoe (Fig 34B) at Reading—an early attempt at increased production. Hoes with a push action were narrow and made of sheet metal (Fig 34C) or socketted (Fig 34D).

Weeds were obviously a problem when there was no chemical means of dealing with them. Besides hoes there were several other tools for dealing with different kinds of weeds. Wooden pliers (Fig 34E) were used for pulling thistles or there were smith-made iron versions (Fig 34F). For large roots there was a fork with footrests (Fig 34G). A variation on this had a piece behind to form a fulcrum for levering a taprooted weed out (Fig 34H). For smaller weeds a narrow hoe was sharpened to cut when pushed and it had a sharpened hook to cut on the pull (Fig 34J).

The two-pronged or three-pronged pitchfork, used for lifting hay, has not changed much (Fig 34K). One with more widely-spaced prongs was used for hedging and lifting brushwood. Multi-pronged forks in wood and iron were used for shovelling hops and other things in brewing. A 'barley pooking fork' was like a pitchfork, but a third prong turned down above the others gathered barley as the fork was pushed along, then this prong could be released to deposit the bundle. Several hooking and poking tools were made like forks. A root pick (Fig 34L) was used by a shepherd for turning swedes and turnips for his sheep. Another hook was used for sheep dipping (Fig 34M) to control his animals. Both of these are from Oxfordshire. The shepherd's crook is a tool of his trade which has varied little from Biblical days.

Wheat and other seeds were planted laboriously in the eighteenth and nineteenth centuries by making holes with wood or metal dibbers (Fig 34N). A man walked backwards using a pair of them to make holes about 4in apart, while others followed dropping in seed and covering over; a team taking about two days to plant an acre.

Other seed was broadcast by hand. The sower had a box hung in front of his waist, called a 'seedlip' and usually made of thin bent wood. Some had a handle for steadying by the hand not sowing (Fig 34P). Sowing broadcast needed considerable skill to get the right density of seed and an even distribution. Several mechanical devices were developed. One that is still used for sowing grass has a box with a sack top to hold the seed, which is allowed to drop in controlled amounts on a star-shaped spreader, rotated in alternate directions by a bow-type handle (Fig 34Q). One was seen in use on the M4 motorway verge in 1972. An American version uses a small crank handle instead of the bow to operate the star-shaped spreader, but is otherwise basically similar. Both are slung from the shoulder by a strap.

When crops cut by a scythe had to be gathered by hand, the rake used was as large as a man could handle (about 5ft). This was called an 'ell rake' or 'drag rake' and fitted with curved iron tines about 3in apart. Unlike the majority of tools, which were ash or other hardwood, the framework was made of softwood and bevelled and rounded as much as possible so as to reduce weight (Fig 35A). A large hooked 'gavel' (Fig 35B) was used to gather cut corn into sheaves.

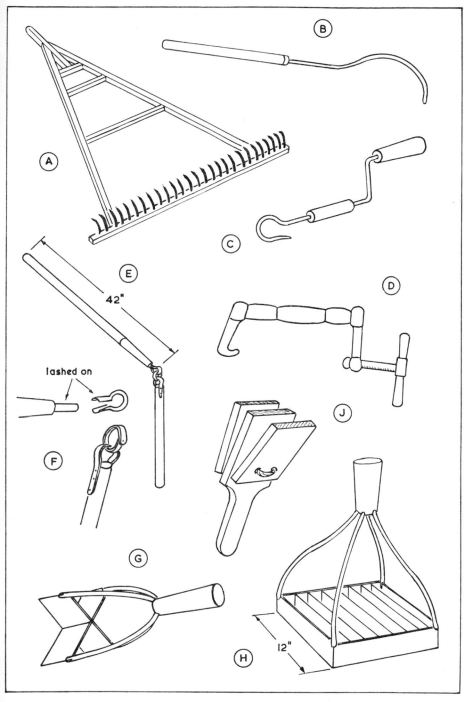

Fig 35 Harvesting tools

Before the days of binder twine, which nowadays seems to be used for everything from securing gates to binding straw bales, trusses of hay had to be bound with rope made from the straw itself. The rope was made by twisting straw with a 'hay bond twister' or 'wimble' ('whimble'). Simplest was a sort of brace made of a piece of iron rod, but a better one had wooden handles, free to rotate on the rod (Fig 35C). A cleverly-made all-wood one is in Cheltenham Museum (Fig 35D). An East Anglian wimble had a loop handle, in which the hook rotated, but this could not have been as efficient as the crank handle. As well as being used in the field, thatchers and others used these tools for making straw rope.

Until the coming of mechanical means of threshing, corn was threshed by hand using a 'flail', which was a pole wielded by another forming a handle, to which it was linked by a universal joint (Fig 35E). Traditionally the handle was ash and the beater or 'swingle' was holly or blackthorn. At the end of the handle was a loop made of ash or yew steamed to shape and lashed on to take the leather link (Fig 35F).

Tools were devised for cutting up root crops. A sort of hoe with crossed blades was pounded up and down to break up turnips and similar things (Fig 35G). Another tool of this type was a 'barley hummeler' (Fig 35H), which was stamped up and down on mown barley to remove the long spines or 'awns' (Somerset name).

One problem in a haystack is the possiblity of spontaneous combustion at the centre. To check the heat at the centre, a long hook was used to thrust into the stack and bring out a few wisps of straw, which were then tested for heat. An example of a compact version, dating from the nineteenth century, has four screwed sections packing into a leather case.

A very important part of the equipment of a man working long hours in the field was a drink container which usually contained cider. Some were neat small barrels, called 'costrels', and good examples of the cooper's skill. Others were earthenware jars. These might hold up to one gallon. The worker carried smaller quantities in a leather bottle or costrel suspended from his belt. Though not a tool the costrel was an important part of a worker's equipment.

Another important tool was the bird scarer, particularly when the owner of the 'big house' maintained a pigeon loft and the consequences of killing pigeons were serious for any of his tenants. All sorts of rattles were used. A simple type had two boards loosely tied each side of a central handled one (Fig 35J).

CHAPTER 14

Fabric and Fibrous Crafts

There are many ancient Greek, Egyptian and Biblical references to cloth making. The interleaving of twigs or rushes in basketwork may have provided the idea, but flax grown in the fields and wool from the sheep's back were the usual weaving materials.

The first step in weaving is the formation of a thread from the raw materials by spinning. Before the coming of the spinning wheel this was done with a spindle, basically a stick with a weight called a 'whorl', to form a flywheel (Fig 36A). The weight was made of stone, pottery, shale, clay or anything that could be made into a heavy wheel shape (Fig 36B). The spindle was up to 2ft long and the whorl was up to 2in diameter. Judging by the number of ancient whorls that have been found in Britain, spinning must have been a universal and constant activity. Similar spindles were used in most parts of the world. An example of a Navaho American Indian spindle was bigger and with a larger wooden whorl (to give sufficient weight with the lighter material). Most spindles were allowed to twirl while suspended, but this larger one had its point on the ground and was turned by rolling along the thigh.

Flax or wool was 'carded'. In the most primitive work this was done by combing tangles out of the wool with teasels—a

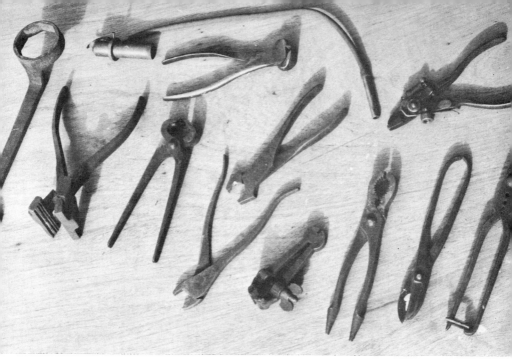

Page 189 (top) Engineering tools: a purpose-made spanner, a spirit blow lamp for soldering and a plier saw set, at the back. Upholsterers' pliers and carpenters' pincers, two nut pliers and a hand vice, pipe plier, tinsnips and a crimping tool for squeezing tube on wire; (*bottom*) using a ball-pane hammer to rivet the blade for a turf cutter

Page 190 (top) A farrier's tool box and tools; (bottom) forge bellows, Vianden, Luxembourg

plant of the sunflower family with prickly heads. The wool was drawn between tied bunches of teasels pulled across each other. In later times teasels were cultivated for this purpose, and their use has not completely died out. For many centuries, until the coming of carding machines in the 1700s, a pair of hand cards were used (Fig 36C). Each had short steel spikes. These are still used by croft weavers in Scotland and elsewhere. Where long stapled wool was needed for making worsted cloth long-toothed combs were used (Fig 36D). Each comb had rows of steel teeth about 9in long, and these had to be kept straight with a metal tube.

Flax was combed by a two-handed 'hatchel' with a circle of stiff wires about 1in high on a 2ft crossbar (Fig 36E).

Wool was loosely rolled as it came off the cards or combs, into lengths with about two-finger thickness. This was gathered on to a distaff, which could be made by pulling together twigs of a suitable branch (Fig 36F). The worker held the base of this under her armpit at one side, while twirling the drop spindle with her other hand.

A spinning wheel is much faster than a spindle and examples from the days when spinning was a serious means of livelihood were much more utilitarian than the ornate wheels made for decoration today. Motive power was a large (4ft), but lightly-built wheel, with a broad rim and turned with a finger against a spoke (Fig 36G). This drove the spindle via a small pulley, the driving belt usually being wool. With the considerable difference in sizes of the wheels, this turned the spindle at quite a high speed (Fig 36H). Wool was fed from a distaff by the hand not turning the wheel.

Driving the wheel by treadle freed both hands. The distaff was mounted on the machine and the wool was fed to the spindle with the aid of a flier (Fig 36J). Women of all grades occupied their time spinning and some of the spinning wheels used by more wealthy ladies were attractive pieces of furniture.

191

M

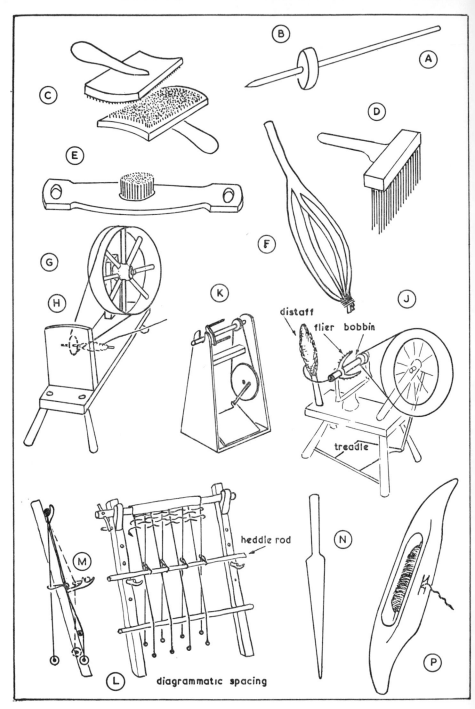

Fig 36 Spinning and weaving equipment

A more basic construction, but similar in effect, was shown in an American pioneer treadle spinner (Fig 36K).

Spinning was a cottage industry; every home producing wool for weaving, until the coming of mechanisation, with the spinning jenny (originally for the cotton industry) near the end of the eighteenth centry, followed by more advanced machines, which took the work away from the home into the factory.

Perhaps surprisingly, judging by present-day experience, little of the wool was used for knitting. Knitting was known, but caps and socks were about the limit of activity. Instead, nearly all the wool went to the loom for weaving.

Looms, of a sort, were known in very early days, as proved by Egyptian paintings. Many ways were used to arrange lengthwise threads ('warp'), so that alternate ones could be lifted to allow the crosswise threads ('weft' or 'woof') to be taken across through the space between ('shed').

An example of a reconstructed Saxon warp-weighted loom is in the Open Air Museum, Singleton, Sussex. A picture on a fourth-century BC Greek vase shows a similar loom. The warp threads hang from a bar, which can turn to roll up the cloth as it is made, and are kept taut by weights, similar to spindle whorls (Fig 36L). The 'heddle rod', looped to alternate threads, may rest against the uprights for one pass of the weft, then is brought out to the 'crotches' to change the warp for the next pass (Fig 36M). Weft threads were knocked up tight by a wooden 'sword' (Fig 36N).

Most weaving by country craftsmen in the Middle Ages was done on a hand loom, with the work horizontal and the warp moved up and down by foot pedals connected to 'reeds' containing wire heddles with holes for the warp threads. The weft thread was wound on a bobbin in a shuttle (Fig 36P), which was thrown across through the shed. Looms of this type are still in use by home and hobby weavers.

Ropemaking

Rope has been made from all kinds of fibres, including human hair. Most of today's rope is made from synthetic fibres, but traditionally it has been made from natural fibres, such as flax, hemp, jute and cotton (particularly in America). Ropemaking can be traced back for at least 2,000 years in Britain, the methods being the same as those used in Egypt many centuries before.

Rope and cordage generally was made by hand in a 'rope walk' up to the middle of the nineteenth century. The first process was very similar to the carding of wool, with the fibres pulled by hand across 'hackle boards', studded with steel pins. A series of these boards had finer pins set closer together, so that finally all fibres were straight and free.

Spinning follows: basically similar to spinning wool. The spinner starts loaded with fibres around his waist and twists some on to a hook at the end of the rope walk. The hook is turned by a crank handle and has a flywheel to keep its speed steady. The spinner walks backwards, adding fibres from his waist, and so builds up a length of 'spun yarn' which is transferred to a reel. This is followed by twisting up into strands in the opposite direction from the twist of the yarns. Strands are twisted together to make rope in the opposite direction from the twist within the strands. Most rope was three-stranded and laid up right-handed (looking along the rope, the strands curve away to the right).

In its simplest form the strands were fixed to three hooks rotated together by a 'fore board' (Fig 37A). The other end was fixed to a single hook and rotated the other way. As the rope would shorten as the strands were twisted, one end had to be movable and could be mounted on a trolley. To assist the twist of the rope and help maintain its evenness, a man in the body of the rope used a sort of wooden club, called a 'woolder' (Fig 37B). Also in the rope walk was a 'top'. This had three grooves

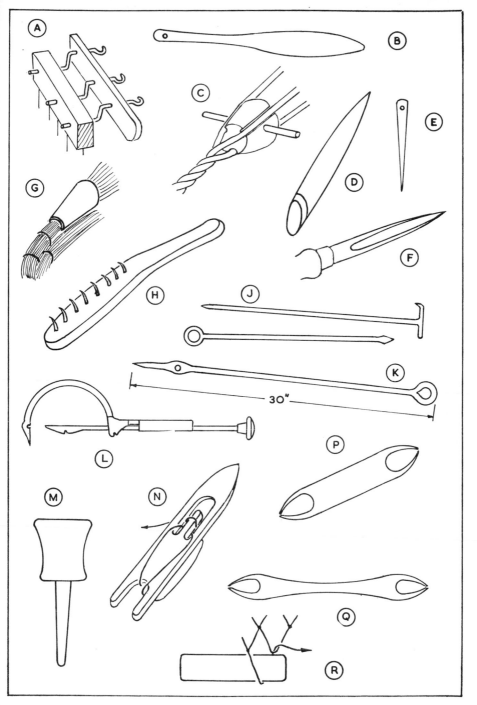

Fig 37 Rope and straw craft tools

(Fig 37C) and was mounted on a cart so that it kept the 'lay' even and progressed along as the rope was built up.

The rigger, or other rope user, had a 'fid' (Fig 37D) for opening rope strands when splicing. This was a hardwood and could be between 6in and 2ft in length. The larger sizes, used on large cable, needed a mallet to drive far enough to open a space for tucking an end strand. For smaller work there was a similar 'marline spike' (Fig 37E) made of steel, up to 6in long, and usually kept on a cord lanyard. Fibre rope stayed open long enough for an end strand to be tucked, but for wire rope, the spike had to be left in to prevent the space closing. A spike had a flat end, so that it could be turned on edge to admit the end strand, or a groove was made in it (Fig 37F) to allow the end strand to slide through. Besom broom makers used a spike, which was often grooved in a similar way, to make a 'road' to tuck ends. They called it a 'bond poker'.

Straw work

Straw, rush and grass were plaited and woven. Knives and other tools for this work have already been described. In the mid-nineteenth century straw was plaited to make hats. Split straws had to be flattened, either by passing a roller over them or by passing between a sort of small mangle, called a 'splint mill'. After plaiting, the finished work was evened up by passing through a 'plait mill' which was like the splint mill, but its rollers were grooved to suit the various sizes of plait.

A lip worker made baskets, bee skeps and other receptacles from bundles of straw, coiled around and sewn together with a binding made by splitting bramble. To open a space for sewing, he used a bone from a horse's hind leg—no wooden or metal awl being considered as suitable. The sizes of the bundles of straws used were regulated by passing through a section of cow horn (Fig 37G).

Besides the cutting, hitting and handling tools already described for his trade, the thatcher had a few peculiar to himself. He used a long straw rake or comb (Fig 37H). This was made of wood and had a few widely-spaced teeth formed from draught nails. It was used for dressing down straw that was laid and for working out loose ends.

The thatcher used a variety of needles, depending on his method. Some were merely pointed skewers (Fig 37J). If the straw was sewn on with tarred twine, he had a large needle with an eye (Fig 37K). As this involved having a second man inside, needles were devised to take care of the inside (Fig 37L).

Chair seating and netmaking

Except for his knife and the means of splitting cane, already described, the cane chair seating craftsman only needed a number of pegs, like steel awls, but with broad tops for tapping in with a mallet (Fig 37M).

Rush seating came into use in the mid-seventeenth century. In the traditional method of weaving the worker needs little equipment besides his knife and some pieces of wood to cram and hit the rush into place. Rush has been followed by rope and seagrass worked in the same way. While rush had to be twisted up as the work progressed the greater length of these other materials calls for some sort of shuttle. In one type (Fig 37N) the line goes around a peg, then through the gap at the end to go around again from the other side and so on. Another type has sprung ends (Fig 37P). For seating, these tools are fairly substantial wood, but similar tools are used for netmaking, and for small mesh nets the slim shuttle or needle is made of metal or bone, and is waisted (Fig 37Q). The netmaker uses a 'mesh stick' (Fig 37R) of the appropriate width to regulate size of mesh.

CHAPTER 15

Other Tools

A few tools that do not conveniently fall into the categories used as headings for earlier chapters are detailed here. Many tools were used in the dairy and kitchen or for other domestic purposes, but their users could not properly be described as country craftsmen. Most of the equipment, such as spits, sugar cutters, fire irons and bins used in the kitchen for the preparation, storage and cooking of food, were the products of local craftsmen, while much of the equipment used in the dairy was also produced locally. Most dairy equipment was made of wood and came from the workshops of the local carpenter and turner.

The farmer used machines of various sorts. Ploughs, seed drills and similar things came in gradually to speed and improve his work. Reapers, threshing machines and other devices progressing up to modern combine harvesters have revolutionised farming, but these things are rather more than craftsmen's tools, and are not therefore within the limits of this book.

While lathes and potters' wheels go back into antiquity and are probably the earliest examples of the use of mechanisation as craftsmen's aids, some of the earliest machines for other purposes must have been mills driven by water or wind power. They came about as the result of craftsmen's skills, but in themselves could not be considered craftsmen's tools.

The power of the wind and water was all that supplemented man's strength when he devised such things as power hammers. The horse also provided power by walking in circles tethered to a central spindle. Horses, ponies and dogs walked inside a wheel to provide power, but in nearly all cases the output was used for drawing water or other domestic purpose and not for use in craftwork. It is interesting to note that when steam power became practicable, the results were judged by comparison with the work done by a horse, and we still quote horsepower today as the unit for rating motors and engines.

Tanners' and Curriers' tools
The preparation of animal skins to make a material suitable for clothing was understood from Paleolithic times, even if the chemistry of it was not as correct and complete as later in history, but the use of oils, alum and oak bark was appreciated centuries ago. Tanneries using oak bark continued until recent times, with comparatively small yards scattered throughout rural Britain. Their place has been taken by large industrial complexes.

The tanner was concerned with the chemical treatment of skins. His work was followed by the currier, who used a variety of tools to prepare the leather for the saddler, bootmaker and other leatherworkers. The tanner had few tools. His 'beamsman' used a large two-handed knife for removing hair (Fig 8R). The man who ground bark for tanning used a fork with more prongs (seven or more) than that used by any other craftsman. Hides treated with lime were cleaned off with a slate-bladed 'scudding knife' or sleaker. The bristles of a pig skin needed a steel 'pig scud' (Fig 38A) to remove them after scalding. This was made like a small garden hoe.

The currier used a sleaker (Fig 8U) to force out dirt, then the hide was 'sammied' by rolling either between a pair of rollers or under a heavy brass roller, needing two men to work

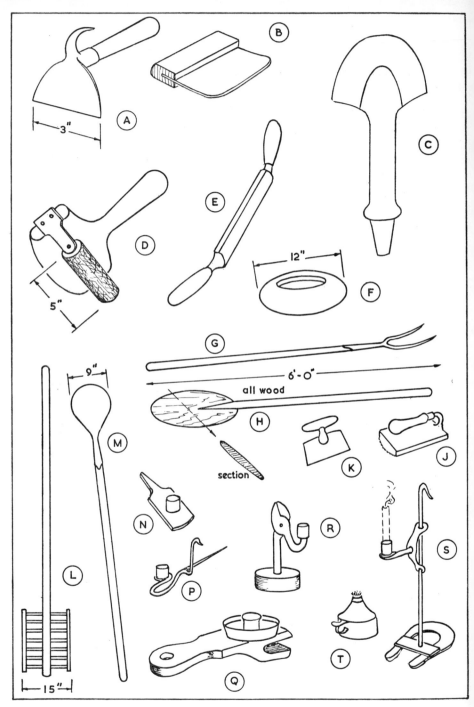

Fig 38 Skin and food tools, lighting

it, on a flat bench top. He then scraped the skin with his special knife (Fig 8V). Sleakers of several sorts were used. A stiff steel blade was used for scraping, but a flexible-bladed tool was used for stretching and was sometimes called a 'stretching tool' (Fig 38B). A stone sleaker had its uses for removing marks from leather. A glass-bladed sleaker was used to press out moisture.

Leather was softened by drawing over a steel 'half-moon stake' (Fig 38C), something like a metalworker's hatchet stake. This was mounted on a block or bench, but a smaller version was used in the hand.

Several tools were used to prepare different surfaces on leather. A pommel (Fig 5E) used cork backed by wood to prepare a waxed surface. A similar tool, but with soft leather in place of the cork, was called a 'sizing pad' and used for finishing calfskins. Metal rollers with grained surfaces were used for special effects (Fig 38D). Another tool, with a burnishing effect, was a two-handled polished steel 'bosher' (Fig 38E), used for polishing shoe upper leather. A 'moon scraper' (Fig 38F) was a slightly conical steel tool with sharp edges used for scraping down sheepskin for making parchment. A similar, but smaller, handled tool was used as an alternative to the pig scud.

Bakers' and brewers' tools

The baker had to deal with a large oven without the aid of thermostats and other controls. He pushed in the bundles of wood faggots to burn and heat the oven with a long light two-pronged fork (Fig 38G) and removed ashes with a rake. Loaves of bread were moved in and out with a slice or 'peel'. Some of these were made of iron and looked like long slender spades, but wood was considered more suitable for use with food and sycamore was popular. The peel blade was not more than $\frac{1}{4}$in thick and tapered to almost nothing around the edges. It was spliced to a handle about 6ft long (Fig 38H). Some bakers had a rasp for removing burnt crust (Fig 38J). The iron surface had raised dots to break away the crust. The farrier used a similar tool on a horse's hoof. For cleaning dough from his mixing trough the baker had a scraper (Fig 38K).

The brewer had to manage a fire, and for this he used larger versions of the smith's slice and rake. He also had to mix and stir in large containers. One mixing tool was a 'mash oar' (Fig 38L). A heavy hardwood one at Charlecote House was described as for 'stirring grist in a mash tun'. Another stirring tool was an iron paddle (Fig 38M) on a long handle, which could have been also used as a baker's peel.

Workshop lighting

The only available artificial lighting was quite feeble, by modern standards, so had to be taken to the job, rather than fixed at a central position. Rush lights gave way to candles and several ingenious holders survive. The candle holder could be on a spike (Fig 38N), possibly with a hook as an alternative fixing (Fig 38P). A wooden holder might clip on the edge of a board (Fig 38Q). For a free-standing holder there had to be a heavy base. A tongs conversion was spiked into a wood block (Fig 38R). The tongs could hold a rush light as an alternative to the candle. Another example took advantage of the weight of a horse shoe (Fig 38S).

Lamps were naked wick affairs, smokily burning various oils, with a wick through a hole or tube (Fig 38T). The coming of lamp glasses and better burning oils gave better illumination in lanterns and standing lamps, while gas was first used in fish-tail burners, then mantles brought a more useful artificial light for the first time. Until the coming of these better means of illumination, precise craftsmanship had to be reserved for day-light hours, while less important jobs were done by artificial light.

Hardening, Tempering and Annealing

Iron cannot be altered in hardness to any appreciable extent by heat treatment or other means. If between 0.5 per cent and 1.5 per cent carbon is added to the iron it becomes 'carbon steel' or 'tool steel'. Today, many other things are added to steel to impart special qualities, but carbon steel can have its hardness varied by heat treatment.

This has been known for a long time, but was imperfectly understood. A sixteenth-century writer advocated: 'Take snayles and first drawn water of a red die, of which water, being taken in the first month of harvest when it raynes, boil it with the snayles, then heat your iron red hot and quench it therein, and it shall be as hard as steel. Ye may do the like with the blood of a man of thirty years of age and of a sanguine complexion, being of a merry nature and pleasant.' His reader would have been disappointed unless what he took to be iron was actually steel, when he would have got the same result with plain water.

If carbon steel is brought to a red heat and allowed to cool slowly it will have the internal stresses due to working 'normalised' and the steel will be in an annealed state, as soft as it can be made. Cooling is best done away from the air, by burying in ashes or something similar.

If the steel is heated to redness and cooled quickly, it becomes hard, possibly almost as hard and brittle as glass, so that a tool would crack or crumble if used. This has been called 'refining', but is more correctly called 'hardening' today. Some of this hardness is removed by a further heat treatment called 'tempering', before the tool is suitable for use. In the quantity-production of tools there are scientific controls of heat, but fortunately for the country tool makers there were rough-and-ready workshop methods that achieved a satisfactory result.

For hardening, steel may be heated to cherry red. Excessive heating is unsatisfactory. It is then quenched quickly. The quicker the cooling, the harder the steel. With quick quenching there is a risk of surface cracks so means may be used to slow the cooling slightly to retain greater toughness without losing any appreciable degree of hardness. Using tepid water is one way. Old-time smiths regarded their own special quenching bath as more important than the amount of heat or speed of cooling.

One way to slow down cooling is to float grease or fat on the water. Tallow, sperm oil and lard oil were used. The hot tool passing through the surface takes some of the fat with it and cooling speed is diminished. Mercury was also used for cooling. To speed cooling and obtain the greatest hardness, salt or sal ammoniac may be added to the water.

To temper the steel for its particular purpose it has to be heated again to a particular temperature and quenched again. This removes some of the hardness, but still leaves the tool much harder than before the first heating. Temperatures for tempering vary between 220°C and 300°C (428°F and 572°F). In the commercial production of tools these temperatures are measured, but for workshop use it is possible to get the correct temperatures by observing colours of oxides on a polished surface of the steel. The effect of air on the heating steel causes coloured films to appear in a definite sequence and at certain temperatures, starting with straw or yellow, deepening to brown, which changes into purple and eventually a dark blue.

The surface of a hardened piece of steel may be rubbed bright with a sandstone. If it is then heated on a metal plate over a flame, the oxide colour can be watched and the steel quenched when the required colour is reached. This is suitable for a tool needing an even tempering all over.

A pointed tool, such as a punch, screwdriver or chisel, may be tempered with a blowlamp. After hardening, the tool is polished for some distance back from the end, then a blowlamp played on the steel several inches back from the end. Heat will travel along the steel toward the end accompanied by the oxides on the polished surface. When the correct colour reaches the end, the tool is quenched. This leaves the body of the tool softer than the cutting end, with some benefit in strength, but the cutting end will only be correctly tempered for about $\frac{1}{2}$in. When this has been sharpened away after use, the tool will have to be hardened and tempered again.

The country smith used either this method of tempering or another method which only needed one heating. In the latter method the pointed tool is heated to redness for several inches back from the point, then the point is quenched by dipping in water. A slight up and down movement prevents an abrupt change between hot and cold on the surface, which might cause cracking. When the point is cold, while the body of the tool is still hot, the point is rubbed bright quickly with a sandstone. Heat from the centre part will move towards the point, and when the correct colour has reached the point, the whole tool is quenched.

The higher the tempering heat before quenching, the softer becomes the steel. Some typical oxide colours are:

Light yellow for metal turning tools

Yellow for engineers' machine tools
Dark yellow for engineers' dies and punches
Brown for engineers' taps, cold chisels
Dark brown for drills, axes, wood chisels, plane irons
Light purple for saws and knives
Dark purple for large saws and screwdrivers
Dark blue for springs.

Copper, brass, aluminium and zinc can only be hardened by working. Hammering to make a bowl, drawing to make wire or passing through rolls, all set up internal stresses and harden the metal. Prolonged working in this way will cause crumbling and cracking. If any of these metals have to be worked extensively, as when forming sheet copper into a deep bowl, frequent annealing is necessary.

Copper is annealed by heating to redness and quenching in water. Brass (an alloy of copper and zinc) may be annealed in the same way, except that sudden cooling may cause cracking, and it is better to let brass cool slowly. Zinc is not much used now, but it was one of the non-ferrous metals available and used for domestic ware before the coming of tinplate and aluminium. Zinc is annealed by heating to about 200°F in hot water. Aluminium is another metal needing little heat to anneal it. Simply smear it with soap and heat over a flame until the soap turns black.

Page 207 (top) Fiddle seed sower—the spreader is rotated by moving the bow; *(bottom)* four-part probe for extracting straw from the middle of a rick to check heat

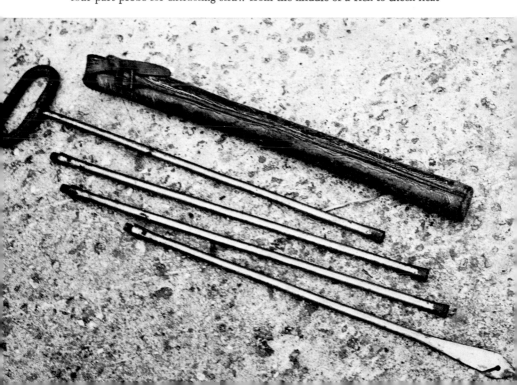

Page 208 (top) Using a wooden fid for splicing rope. A knife and a wire-splicing spike are alongside; (bottom) sharpening a plane iron on an oilstone, with a gouge slip in the foreground

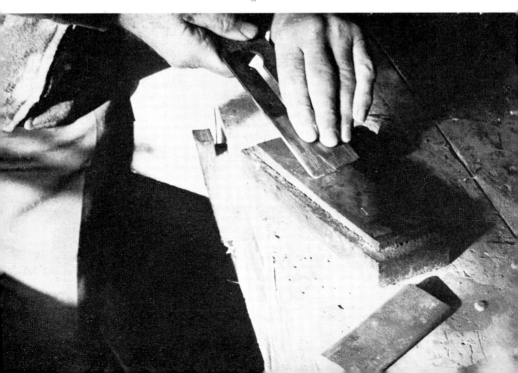

APPENDIX 2

Tool Sharpening

Although it is possible to put a sharp edge on a tool made of almost any material, it is obvious that a soft material would crumble at the first attempt to cut with it, so sharpening as an operation is tied up with the material used in the tool. With early stone tools it was a matter of luck, but primitive craftsmen soon found that some stones were much harder than others and some could be cracked or chipped to give an edge sufficiently strong to stand up to frequent use. The discovery of bronze and then iron gave the craftsman some control over the choice of material used, but his tools were still comparatively soft and unable to take a fine cutting edge that could be expected to last. It was not until the development of steel, made by adding carbon to iron, that hardening and tempering became possible (see Appendix 1) and tools could be given sharp cutting edges that would last.

Sharpening is the wearing away of the edge of a steel tool until both surfaces meet at a point of no thickness. In fact, because of the nature of the material, there must be a minute thickness left, but with modern alloy steels the thickness is infinitesimal and an exceptionally keen edge is possible, as in modern stainless steel razor blades.

The angle of the cutting edge is governed by the use of the

Fig 39 Tool sharpening

tool. For a knifelike cut, the more acute the angle, the sharper it will be, but there will be little strength. It is, of course, the angle at the cutting edge which counts and not any angle in the tool further back in the blade. Open razors were 'hollow ground' (Fig 39A) to allow for the edge being given a very acute angle, without metal back from the edge interfering with sharpening. Such a fine angle would not last long for cutting wood, so a knife or chisel-type tool has to sacrifice some sharpness for the sake of strength and be given a cutting angle about 15° (Fig 39B). If the tool is to be used with a swing, as in an axe, the cutting angle has to be slightly more obtuse, particularly for hardwoods. For cutting metal there has to be a greater concession to strength and the angle opens to about 60° (Fig 39C). A more acute angle can be used for soft metals or for cutting iron softened by heating.

Tools are sharpened by rubbing steel away with an abrasive grit. A coarse grit tends to wear away steel quicker than a fine grit of the same type. The effect of the grit is to produce a sawlike edge, with the size of the 'teeth' matching the size of the grit. Consequently, an edge produced by a coarse grit will have a rougher and less sharp edge than one produced with a fine grit (Fig 39D). Of course, the roughness of an edge that has been made by a coarse grit might be too fine to be visible to the naked eye.

From quite early days it was realised that coarse grits cut fast and fine grits produced the sharpest edges, so sharpening was best done in two stages. Sandstone was the most readily available coarse grit. Steel was worn away by rubbing on it. Water aided sharpening and prevented the stone becoming clogged with minute particles of steel. Knife sharpening on a cottage doorstep may still be seen. A sandstone made into a wheel and mounted on an axle with a handle became the accepted grindstone and is still preferred to smaller high-speed manufactured grinding stones for woodworkers' tools (Fig 39E). Water was used on the stone, both to aid sharpening and to keep the tool cool so that its temper would not be drawn.

While the sandstone wheel removed metal fairly quickly, a finer stone was needed to reduce the coarse serrations on the edge and replace them with finer ones. Natural stones of suitable fine grit were treasured, as their finding might be due to luck, although certain stones were quarried and distributed under various names. 'Water of Ayr' and 'Turkey' stones were natural grits made into sharpening stones. The finer sharpening stone was lubricated with water—often spittle—or oil. Neat's foot oil, obtained from the hooves of ox or cow, was one favourite. Nowadays any fine lubricating oil is used, but until quite recent times craftsmen kept their own special choice of oil for sharpening. As water and oil will not mix, one or the other had always to be used. The men in the field used water, while the craftsman at the bench favoured oil.

An alternative to using a sharpening stone is to use an abrasive in grit or sand form. Fine abrasive mixed with oil could be used on a piece of glass, with the chisel or similar tool rubbed on it. In the field, a wooden tool, called a 'riff' (Fig 39F), was smeared with grease and sprinkled with sand or coated with wet sand from a ditch and the tool rubbed on it. The tool had to be drawn across or the riff rubbed on it with a stroking action over the edge, as the other way would make the tool cut into the wood.

For the finest edge, stones of successively finer grit were used —each removing the serrations made by the earlier one. One effect of using very fine sharpening stones is to leave a tiny particle of steel clinging to the edge, called a 'wire edge' or 'dingle edge' (Fig 39G). The presence of this indicates that the two surfaces are meeting and the tool is sharp. It can sometimes be seen, but if too fine to see, it can be felt by wiping a finger lightly from the body of the tool over the edge, when it will be felt curling to one side.

The wire edge has to be removed. A chisel or plane iron can be sliced across a piece of wood. Another way is to strop it, by stroking several times from both sides on a piece of leather. The barber does this with a razor on a piece of leather held by hand tension, but a craftsman had leather, dressed with oil to keep it supple, glued to a piece of wood.

Whether the tool is rubbed on the sharpening stone or the stone on the tool, the effect should be the same. With a shaped tool, like a sickle or scythe, the sharpening stone, sometimes called a 'whetstone' or 'rubber', was used like a file on opposite sides of the blade in turn. The rubber, once natural, but now manufactured, was oval in section and thicker near the middle (Fig 39H). An experienced user sharpened with an extremely quick action, drawing the stone across and along each side of the blade alternately. A tool of the scythe type depends on the keenness of the blade, so frequent sharpening was necessary and the stone was carried in a sheath on the belt. Sharpening in this way was referred to as 'whetting', not 'wetting'.

In some tools the sharpening angle obtained by grinding is followed by stones of finer grits at the same angle, so that the final finish has an even smooth slightly curved slope from the body of the tool to the edge. This occurs in most knives and axes and is favoured for carving and turning tools (Fig 39J). Other tools, such as ordinary chisels and plane irons, are sharpened with two bevels. The 'grinding bevel' takes off the bulk of the surplus metal, then the 'sharpening bevel' produces the cutting edge on a finer stone (Fig 39K). These tools are sharpened on one side, preferably with a figure-eight action over the whole surface of the stone, to wear it evenly (Fig 39L), then the edge is rubbed flat on the other side (Fig 39M) to remove or loosen the wire edge. For straight-edged cutting tools the oilstone needs to be flat. A natural stone was worked level by rubbing against another stone or by rubbing on a sheet of glass covered with abrasive grit. It was mounted in wood and a cover fitted.

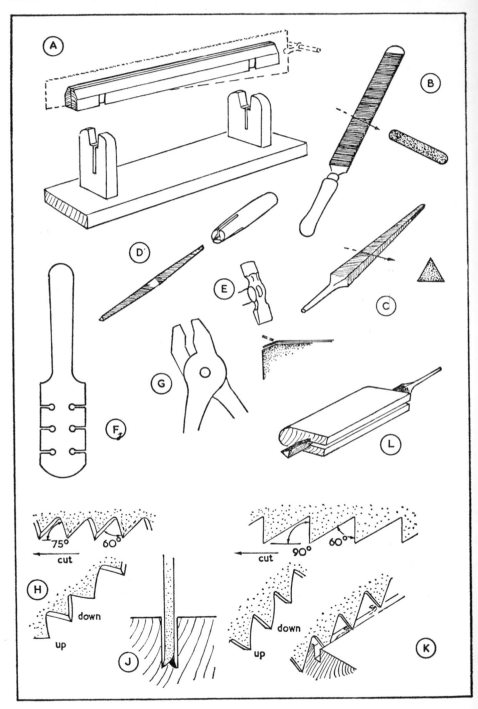

Fig 40 Saw teeth and saw sharpening

The insides of gouges and other curved tools had to be sharpened with a 'slip stone' (Fig 39N), which was a piece of oilstone rounded on the edge and used in the hand like a file.

Saw sharpening was regarded as something of a craft mystery, in the same way that other craft practices were kept to those who had served an apprenticeship. A sawyer sharpened his pit saws and might sharpen saws for other craftsmen, or one man in a workshop would be the 'saw doctor' and keep saws in trim for other workers.

For sharpening, a saw was held in a vice, often two strips of wood held in two uprights by a wedge action (Fig 40A). For the finer saws there were metal versions of this, with a screw or lever action. Sharpening was with a file. For large teeth there was a 'mill file' about 10in long and with a cross-section having rounded edges (Fig 40B). In some cases a half-round file was used. For small teeth the file was of regular triangular cross-section and called a 'three-square file' (Fig 40C). These files, on tempered saw blades, soon became blunt and later ones were made double-ended to have a longer life, with a special split handle (Fig 40D). Saw files were single-cut (teeth in single lines, instead of the usual two crossing lines).

Saw teeth had to be set before they were sharpened. Alternate teeth were bent in opposite directions, so as to cut a 'kerf' wider than the thickness of the saw and reduce binding on a deep cut. This could be done with a cross-pane hammer over an anvil edge (Fig 40E). For very fine teeth or when the craftsman could not trust himself to hit the correct tooth every time, a punch was put on the tooth and hit by a hammer. While hitting was the only satisfactory way of setting small teeth, large teeth could be levered with a notched 'saw set' (Fig 40F). Plier-type 'saw sets' were devised to do the same job, particularly on finer saws (Fig 40G).

Because of the fibrous nature of wood a saw tooth has to cut like a knife across the grain, while it needs more of a chisel action along the grain. For cross-cutting, teeth were filed so that each cut on the outside of its set (Fig 40H). In use this meant that the set teeth severed two lines of wood fibre each side of the kerf (Fig 40J). A 'rip saw' for cutting along the grain had its teeth filed straight across, so that every tooth acted something like a little plane (Fig 40K).

The 60° of the three-square file settled the angles of teeth it was used on. For the very large teeth of a pit saw, the mill file permitted other angles, but the included angle between the face of one tooth and the back of the next was usually about 60°. The rounded edge of the file allowed the bottom of the 'gullet' between teeth to be rounded, which minimised the risk of the steel cracking there. Until fairly modern times the teeth of British cross-cut saws intended for green wood relied on coarse teeth to clear sawdust, but more recent saws show an American influence with groups of teeth separated by deep gullets to remove sawdust. These had to be filed deeper with a round file, as tooth sharpening reduced the width of the saw.

A saw cuts much better and is easier to control if all teeth are the same height. Early saws had very uneven teeth, but more recent saw sharpeners 'top' the teeth before sharpening by rubbing with a flat file held in the hand or with a file mounted in a wooden guide (Fig 40L). With the tops of the teeth level, even if then of uneven size, filing can be done to bring the points back into shape and all to the same heights.

APPENDIX 3

Timber

Wood was, and still is, the most commonly used material employed by craftsmen. There are some general characteristics of timber, which distinguish it from other materials, but there are many sorts of wood, with their own characteristics and qualities which have been learned by experience, and a craftsman is able to select a particular type of tree to suit his purpose and even pick parts of the same tree for qualities he wants.

Nearly all trees, and certainly the ones used for timber, are exogenous or outward growing. They increase in girth year by year. Each year an 'annual ring' is formed outside those already there (Fig 41A). By counting the rings of a cross-section of a felled tree it is possible to determine its age.

Trees are broadly divided into 'hardwoods' and 'softwoods'. While being correct descriptions for many woods, the names are rather misleading as some hardwoods are softer than some softwoods. The term 'hardwood' is given to a tree that has broad leaves, while a 'softwood' tree has needle leaves. In nearly all cases the hardwood tree sheds its leaves in the winter, while the softwood tree keeps its needles. Hardwoods are mostly much slower growers than softwoods.

In the cross-section of the tree the older wood near the centre tends to be harder and more durable than the newer wood.

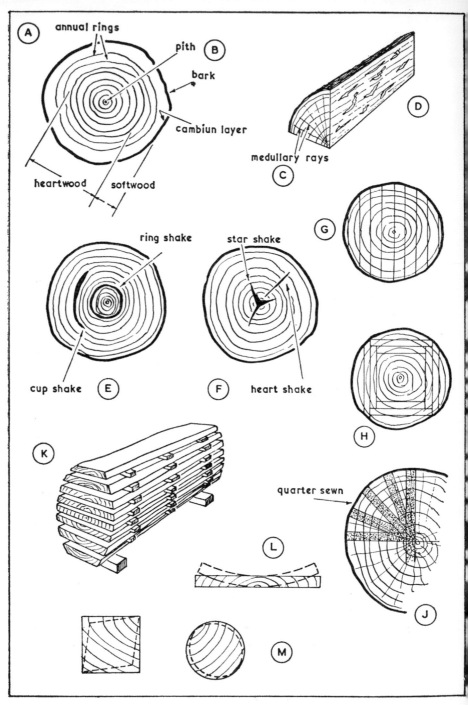

Fig 41 Timber cutting and seasoning

This is the 'heartwood' and the outer wood, which is wetter with sap, is called 'sapwood'. The original centre of the sapling, which started the tree, is the 'pith' (Fig 41B). In an old tree this is so small and compressed as to be insignificant. It is the heartwood that is of value for timber. Sapwood lacks durability and strength. Outside of the sapwood is the 'cambium layer' which represents growth and gives birth to new annual rings. Around it all is the bark, which is no use as timber, but it has other uses in some trees, including tanning and corkmaking.

There are radial lines of cells, called 'medullary rays' passing through the annual rings (Fig 41C). In some trees they are easily seen, but in many trees they can only be seen under a glass. They are particularly prominent in oak and when a cut is made radially they are seen as 'figured' or 'wainscot' oak (Fig 41D).

A tree does not grow as a regular cylinder, with true circular section and straight sides, but its irregular shape gives the differences in grain form which makes the attractive appearance and sometimes allows for cutting to follow the lines of grain, giving greater strength than if the cut severs lines of grain.

Where branches grow from the trunk the point of union makes a knot in a cut plank. Forest trees have straighter trunks and are freer from branches, and therefore knots, than trees growing in the open, where they do not have to grow upwards to hold their own with other trees in reaching towards sunlight.

During its life a tree may develop lengthwise cracks, called 'shakes'. If they follow the annual rings they are 'cup' or 'ring' shakes (Fig 41E). A single crack across is a 'heart' shake, while several crossings are 'star' shakes (Fig 41F). Shakes affect the value of a tree as timber and may not be apparent until it is felled. Some other defects are sought after. In particular, the excrescence known as 'burr' on some hardwood trees can be cut to give an attractive effect, particularly as veneers.

For economy a tree is cut across into boards (Fig 41G). These boards will be marked by the grain in different ways and will have different resistance to stress and warping. If it is the marking of grain that is important, some woods are cut squarely around the tree (Fig 41H), but this results in some waste. If it is oak being cut for figuring, the boards have to be cut radially ('quarter sawn') on the lines of the medullary rays (Fig 41J) and this is more wasteful and consequently more expensive.

Trees are usually felled and cut into boards thicker than will eventually be required, so that they can be stacked for 'seasoning'. Newly-cut timber contains a considerable amount of water, with other things in solution. Most of this has to be removed before the timber can be used. The timber is not satisfactory for working or for construction until the moisture content is down to an acceptable figure, which varies, but is between 6 per cent and 30 per cent.

Natural seasoning was practised by the country craftsmen. The sawn boards were stacked with spacers so that air could circulate (Fig 41K). Protection is provided from extremes of weather, but otherwise the wood is able to dry out in normal atmospheric conditions. This is a slow process, with timber having to lay for a year or more before it is fit to use. Modern methods hasten the process, but kiln drying and other quick methods were not available to the country craftsman, and probably would not have been accepted by him. Natural seasoning is still regarded as the best, when time and space can be found.

Wood swells and shrinks unequally as it dries or re-absorbs moisture. A board cut across the centre of a tree may swell or shrink, but is unlikely to warp. One cut further out may warp in the direction of the annual rings (Fig 41L). A square or circle will shrink in the direction of the grain (Fig 41M) if the shape is cut before the timber has dried. Timber does not expand and contract much in the length, although a plank may twist or go 'into winding'.

The country craftsman found a use for most woods that grew in his locality, but by far the most widely-used wood was oak, for structural work, furniture making and almost anything required. Elm, ash and beech were other hardwoods also widely distributed and therefore used for many things, although they were more suitable for specialised jobs. Nowadays softwoods are grown as a comparatively quick crop in many parts of Britain, but until their coming as a cultivated wood within the last century, softwoods did not find much place in the work of a country craftsman.

There are several varieties of oak, but that common to Britain is usually called 'English oak'. It is dark brown, with a rather coarse grain of even colour and the medullary rays are more prominent than in other woods. It is extremely durable. Oak-framed houses 500 years old are in existence with the wood still in hard and sound condition. English oak is mostly too coarse for fine work and there is evidence that milder oak from elsewhere has been imported as far back as the Middle Ages for better quality furniture. Oak trees can grow quite high in forests, but most that were used for country crafts were low with spreading branches, yielding broad planks of no great length.

Elm trees were, and still are, a common feature of the British landscape, although elm disease has caused the removal of many of them. Elm has a twisted grain giving it a more even strength in all directions, with little risk of splintering or cracking. This makes it suitable for wheel hubs and chair seats. Elm can produce wide boards, but with some tendency to twist and warp. Floors of old houses are often uneven due to the boards being elm. Elm stands up to damp conditions. Indeed, it was used for water pipes and parts exposed to the weather. Because of its twisted grain, elm did not respond to cleaving and all wood had to be sawn.

Ash is mainly a hill tree, but it grows almost anywhere, although not to a great size. The wood is hard and fairly straight-grained, with a grey colour and even grain markings. Ash is strong and resilient. It could be cleft or sawn. No other British wood was as good for cart shafts or the handles of hammering-type tools where the wood had to stand up to bending and twisting stresses. It was also used for hurdles and ladder poles. It responded to steaming and could be shaped into scythe sneathes or other curved handles as well as the frameworks of waggon covers and, later, motor van bodies.

Beech, another commonly-used wood in country crafts, has a close even grain, of reddish-brown colour. It is stable, with little risk of splitting or variations due to changes in atmospheric conditions. However, it is not durable and cannot be relied on to last in outdoor structures. Planes, mallet heads and similar tools were made almost exclusively of beech. It turns well and was thus popular for chisel handles and most turned ware. Beech was also grown specially for chairmaking—the trees being planted close so as to grow straight and tall.

The foregoing woods were the mainstay of general woodworking in country workshops. Other woods are listed below, not in order of popularity or importance, but in alphabetical order.

Hardwoods

Alder became more of a coppice wood, although it can grow into a substantial tree. The wood is pale and soft, with little grain marking. Alder grown in bogs becomes darker and this had some use for furniture making. The ordinary wood had some popularity for turned articles and was used also for clogs.

Birch tends to be slender, so does not produce boards of much useful width. The brown wood is rather coarse and was used for making small articles only. Its twigs were used for besom brooms. In recent years birch has been used as veneer for making plywood.

Box is a tree which grows very slowly and does not reach much size. It is very dense and stable. Its wood is yellow and with little grain marking. Small tools, rules and straight-edges of box keep their size and shape. Box was the popular wood for engraving, and it was used for very fine and detailed turned work. It was also turned for better-quality carving tool handles. Trees were not widely found and the wood was prized for its particular qualities.

Sweet chestnut is a wood that looks like oak without the prominent medullary rays. It was little used as a benchwork timber, but was cleft for fencing and hurdles. Young trees were used as poles for scaffolding and supporting hops.

Hazel is rarely seen as a benchwork timber, but was coppice grown for making wattle hurdles and baskets. Pegs and other parts used in thatching were also made from it.

Holly, when allowed to grow into a tree, produces a close-grained near-white wood, suitable for many uses similar to box. It turns well. Shuttles for hand weaving were made of holly.

Hornbeam is a rather uncommon tree, but its virtue is in producing the hardest British wood, used instead of beech to make stronger planes and other tools. Hornbeam stood up to use as cogs in wind and water mills. Screw threads could be cut in it.

Lime was more of a decorative tree in landscaping and parkland, but its light-coloured wood is easily cut and it had some popularity with carvers.

Poplar was no use for any object required to last, but it was used in dry coopering, making casks for vegetables and similar things.

Sycamore was not plentiful in southern England, but was long established in Wales and Northern Britain. With its near-white close grain it is a clean-looking wood for domestic ware, which does not impart taste or smell to food. It turns well. Rollers for domestic mangles and similar purposes were made of sycamore.

Walnut was grown for decoration and for the nuts, but its timber was used for furniture. It has a bold red-brown grain. Burrs are formed on walnut trees and can be cut across to produce attractive grain markings. Walnut was sawn into veneers to fix to other woods. It is the wood regarded as the most shock-absorbent and suitable for gun stocks.

Willow is one of the 'hardwoods' which is actually soft. There are several varieties. Its best-known use today is probably in making cricket bats, but it was also used for gate hurdles and basketmaking. The clean white soft wood has little use as a structural or furniture timber.

Fruit trees were grown firstly for their fruit. When felled they yielded close-grained nicely-marked timber of no great size, but apple, pear and similar woods were used for making small articles of attractive appearance.

Softwoods

Most softwoods today are imported, although Scots Pine is now grown as a crop in many parts of Britain. This wood was used in the pole as masts and pit props. It could be cleft to make ladder sides, being lighter than ash, although not as durable.

Spruce is more common in Europe than in Britain where it had uses similar to Scots Pine. It is lighter and even better for cleaving, so could be used for barrel staves, hoops and basket-making. Spruce does not warp, even when thinly cleft. This made it suitable for the slats of Venetian blinds. It also had a use in the making of instruments of the violin family.

Larch was introduced into Britain from Europe in the sixteenth century. This tough, strong wood was used for fencing and gates and for boat planking and frames.

Yew, a hard 'softwood', has always had something of a super-stitious tradition. It was used mainly for making bows, but as the seeds and possibly the leaves are poisonous to cattle it had to be kept from them, so yew trees were often grown for bow making in church yards. They may still be found there. Yew was used for barrel hoops. It was also bent into the bow backs of Windsor chairs.

APPENDIX 4

Craft Names

The names of many trades and crafts are the same today as they have been for hundreds of years and most people are familiar with the scope of activities embraced by a particular name, but some trades have disappeared as the need for them has gone, and their names are now unfamiliar. Other names have different meanings, or the craftsmen using the names are now engaged in rather different activities, possibly because of the need to move with the times and make use of improved methods if the demand for their skill were to be maintained.

Some trades overlap. One man may have had several skills and been employed in different spheres as the need arose, for there was insufficient call for a particular skill as a fulltime job in many small communities. In any case, almost every man had a stake in the land and raised crops or animals in addition to practising his trade. For the more established and major crafts there were guilds controlling them, with membership jealously guarded. Although these might be loosely compared with trades unions today, their members were more often self-employed individuals. The guilds were concerned with quality of workmanship as much as with the returns from practising the craft.

As an aid to readers unfamiliar with the names of crafts and related terms an alphabetical list, with notes, is given below:

Apprentice. For most trades a boy was expected to serve an apprenticeship, usually of seven years, during which time he agreed to certain terms and the master agreed to teach him the trade. In many cases the boy lived with the master.

Architect. This is a comparatively new name. The nearest traditional name is 'Master Mason' for the man who supervised the building work.

Arrowsmith. The maker of arrow heads.

Basketmaker. This term covered those who wove withies or straw and those who made baskets from thin wood. See 'Lipworker', 'Spale basketmaker' and 'Trugger'.

Benchman. A sub-division of chairmaking. He sawed the parts to shape, including any fretted work.

Bender. A sub-division of chairmaking. He shaped the bent parts for Windsor and other chairs.

Besom broom maker. See 'Broom squire'.

Blacksmith. One of the longest established trade names. He worked hot iron and this name was used instead of 'smith' when necessary to distinguish his trade from that of the 'whitesmith'.

Bodger. See 'Chair bodger'.

Bootmaker. The maker of all-leather footwear, but he may also have been a 'Clogger'.

Bottomer. A sub-division of chairmaking. He followed the benchman and used an adze to shape chair seats.

Bowl turner. The specialist turner of wooden bowls, usually on a pole lathe.

Bowmaker or Bowyer. The maker of long bows.

Brewer. Most villages had a brewery for producing ale and beer, and some farms had their own brewery.

Brickmaker. Before mechanisation in the nineteenth century, bricks were moulded individually from local clay, the brickmaker often travelling to places where houses were being built.

Broom squire. The maker of besom brooms.

Brushmaker. Any maker of brushes, but most were 'broom squires'.

Cabinetmaker. The woodworker who made the more advanced type of furniture, of better quality than that produced by a 'carpenter'.

Caner. The maker of cane chair seats.

Carpenter. A general term for a woodworker, but particularly meaning the man who made fences, gates, stiles, general wood-work and basic cottage furniture. He might also make coffins and act as undertaker.

Carver. See 'Woodcarver'.

Chair bodger. The craftsman using a pole lathe set up in wood-land who made chair legs and rails.

Chairmaker. A general term covering the making of chairs, but sub-divided into 'Benchman', 'Bottomer', 'Bender', 'Framer' and 'Finisher'. The trade also embraced 'Chair bodger' and 'Caner'.

Charcoal burner. Itinerant craftsman who lived in the woods to control their slow-burning fires.

Clogger or Clogmaker. In Britain clogs had wooden soles and leather uppers. The name was used for the man who worked in the forest cutting and roughly trimming wooden soles, and for the man who completed the job. He might also be a 'Boot-maker'.

Coachbuilder or Coachmaker. The maker of passenger-carrying vehicles, as distinct from the waggons of the 'wheelwright'.

Cobbler. A boot repairer, rather than a maker, but not a very acceptable name.

Cooper, dry. The maker of casks and barrels for holding powders, vegetables and dry goods. Not as skilled as a 'Wet Cooper'.

Cooper, wet. The maker of casks and barrels for liquids.

Coracle builder. The maker of craft consisting of basketwork structures covered with canvas or skin.

Cordwainer. A preparer of sheep skins for fine leather. The name is from Cordova in Spain, where these craftsmen were exceptionally skilful.

Cottage industries. See 'Outworkers'.

Currier. The craftsman who followed the 'Tanner' and worked the leather with tools.

Doorman. The 'Farrier's' helper or mate.

Dry cooper. See 'Cooper'.

Dry stone waller. Builder of stone walls without cement or other jointing material.

Engineer. Not a traditional trade name until the Industrial Revolution.

Farrier. The maker and fitter of horse shoes, sometimes also a 'Blacksmith' and often with some veterinary knowledge.

Fellmonger. The dealer in skins and hides, who bought them from slaughterhouses or farms and sold them to the 'Tanner'.

Finisher. A sub-division of chairmaking. He finished off the woodwork of an assembled chair, then stained and polished it.

Fletcher. Strictly, the man who feathered arrows, but he usually also made them.

Flint knapper. He prepared flint for use in striking a light or in a fire-arm.

Forester. General name for a worker in the forest, but in particular the more skilled forest worker who took charge of work and planned planting and tree management.

Foundryman. The worker who cast metals, usually iron. See also 'Moulder'.

Framer. A sub-division of chairmaking. The craftsman who assembled chairs after parts had been prepared by 'Benchman', 'Bottomer' and 'Bender'.

Free Mason. A mason who worked as a sub-contractor instead of for a wage.

Gate hurdlemaker. The maker of hurdles of gatelike pattern, with cleft wood parts tenonned together. See also 'Wattle hurdlemaker'.

Glazier. One who made and fixed the glass parts of windows.

Harnessmaker. See 'Saddler'.

Hedger and ditcher. An agricultural craftsman who interwove the parts of a growing hedge and made or cleared drainage ditches.

Hewer. An early name for the man who quarried and first prepared stone for the mason.

Hoopmaker. A craft usually carried out in the open, making hoops for dry barrels.

Horner. A worker in animal's horns.

Hurdlemaker. The maker of portable hurdle fencing, mainly used for enclosing sheep and divided into two trades: 'Gate hurdlemaking' and 'Wattle hurdlemaking'.

Improver. In many trades a man who had completed his apprenticeship spent a further year, or other period, as an improver before being accepted as a 'journeyman'.

Indentures. The document setting out the agreement between apprentice and master.

Joiner. A fairly recent name for a specialist branch of woodworking, generally considered more skilled than carpentry, and including such work as all kinds of window frames, doors and shop fittings. Many carpenters described themselves as 'carpenter and joiner'.

Journeyman. A fully-qualified craftsman, accepted as such by a guild, if one existed. The name came from the fact that a man was expected to journey and broaden his experience before settling. A journeyman was employed rather than a master craftsman.

Knapper. See 'Flint knapper'.

Lacemaker. See 'Pillow lacemaker'.

Laddermaker. The maker of wooden ladders, who usually practised another wood craft as well.

Layer. An early name for a rough mason, who followed the work of a 'Hewer', but was not as skilled as a 'Mason'.

Lipworker. A basketmaker using bundles of straw bound with bramble or cane. 'Lip' comes from the Scandinavian 'lob', meaning coiled basketry. A particular product was a bee hive or skep.

Mason. A worker in stone, particularly one who carved or otherwise decorated stone.

Master mason. The designer and supervisor of a stone building, very similar to a present-day 'Architect'.

Millwright. The craftsman who built and maintained the mechanical parts of wind and water mills. The name continued to be used in industry for the man responsible for the maintenance of factory machinery.

Moulder. The foundryworker who prepared the sand moulds into which molten metal was poured.

Navvy. A labourer with pick and shovel. Canals were first called 'navigations' and those who dug them were 'navigators', which became shortened to 'navvy'.

Osier basketmaker. The maker of baskets from osiers (withie, willow) by interweaving the split lengths.

Outworkers. Those who did work in their own homes away from a central workshop. Their work was sold, and sometimes completed, by someone else.

Painter. Except for very specialised decoration, painting was not regarded as a country trade and was done by other craftsmen.

Patternmaker. The maker of wooden patterns used to prepare sand moulds for metal castings.

Pillow lacemaker. A worker who made lace on a pillow with bobbins. Needlepoint and some other lace was made without a pillow.

Plaiter. See 'Straw plaiter'.

Potter. An old craft. The name is usually applied to one who spun clay on a wheel, but could also be applied to other workers in clay.

Rakemaker. A specialist in making all-wood rakes.

Ropemaker. A specialist in the making of rope and cordage.

Saddler. A skilled worker in leather, making all parts of harness as well as saddles and other leather goods.

Saw doctor. Not usually a trade in itself, but the name given to the craftsman who undertook the sharpening of saws.

Sawyer. Anyone who sawed wood, but particularly those who converted logs with a pit saw.

Scythemaker. One who shaped scythe sneaths and assembled scythes. This might be combined with laddermaking or other woodworking craft.

Slatter, slater. A craftsman who split and prepared slates for roofing. Also applied to the man who fixed them.

Smith. A worker with hot iron or steel, but with the coming of the name 'Whitesmith' this had to be qualified as 'Blacksmith'.

Spale basketmaker. The maker of baskets from thin pieces of oak in a pattern peculiar to the North and Midlands of England. Very similar to 'Trugger'.

Spinner. A very old activity, almost exclusive to women, preparing wool as received from sheep shearing, so that it could be wound on bobbins for weaving. In more recent days the name is given to a craftsman using a lathe to form sheet metal into bowl and cup shapes.

Spoonmaker. A particularly Welsh activity, making wooden spoons. Often associated with bowl turning and loosely described as turnery.

Stone mason. See 'Mason'.

Straw plaiter. A man or woman who prepared straw for the making of hats and similar things.

Tailor. The maker of men's outer clothing.

Tanner. The worker who treated a hide chemically as the first step after receiving it from the slaughterhouse and before passing it to the 'Currier'.

Thatcher. The craftsman using straw or reed to roof a house.

He might thatch a rick, but this was more often done by the farm worker.

Tinsmith. A usually itinerant worker who repaired tinplate pots and pans.

Tree feller. See 'Woodman'.

Turner. A craftsman who operates a lathe.

Trugger. The maker of baskets from thin pieces of willow in a pattern peculiar to southern England. The name is from old English 'trog' meaning tub or boat. Very similar to 'Spale basketmaking'.

Waller. See 'Dry stone waller'.

Wattle hurdlemaker. A craftsman who made hurdles by weaving hazel and similar strips. See also 'Gate hurdlemaker'.

Weaver. The operator of a loom, of any sort.

Webster. Early name for 'Weaver'.

Wet cooper. See 'Cooper'.

Wheelwright. A specialist woodworker, who made waggons as well as wheels.

Whitesmith. A metalworker mainly concerned with plumbing and usually embracing tinsmithing. The name distinguishes him from a 'Blacksmith'.

Woodcarver. A decorative woodworker, using a large range of chisels and gouges to form stylised or natural designs in wood.

Woodman, woodcutter. The general worker in forest or coppice, cutting and felling trees.

Wood turner. A worker who used a lathe to turn wood. Usually just a 'Turner' unless it is necessary to distinguish him from a turner of other materials.

Wool stapler. A trader in wool in its raw state.

Bibliography

There have been many books about craftwork in general and about particular crafts, but many of these are long out of print and not easily obtainable. The following short list includes books which the author considers particularly relevant to the subject of tools and which are obtainable through booksellers or libraries.

GENERAL

Crafts of the Countryside E. J. Stowe (Longmans 1948)

Country Craftsmen Freda Derrick (Chapman & Hall 1945)

A History of Everyday Things in England Marjorie and C. H. B. Quennell 5 vols (Batsford 1959)

The Shell Book of Country Crafts James Arnold (John Baker 1970)

Traditional Country Crafts J. Geraint Jenkins (Routledge & Kegan Paul 1966)

Woodland Crafts in Britain Herbert L. Edlin (1949; repr David & Charles 1973)

PARTICULAR

The Blacksmith's Craft (Rural Industries Bureau 1952)

British Coracles and Irish Curraghs J. Hornell (Quaritch 1938)

Bibliography

Handcraft in Wood and Metal J. Hooper & A. J. Shirley (Batsford 1931)

The History of Chair Making in High Wycombe Mayes (Routledge & Kegan Paul 1960)

The Thatcher's Craft (Rural Industries Bureau 1961)

Tools and Devices for Coppice Crafts Young Farmers' Club Booklet 31 (Evans 1957)

Tools and Supplies Catalogue (Buck & Hickman 1958)

Index

Illustrations are indicated by italics

Index